More comments on "The Prediction Trap":

"The Parrot Principle discussed in *The Prediction Trap* is especially demonic in the world of economics, and as an economist, I can attest that it's an easy trap to fall into. We economists talk so freely about all kinds of things, and if they are said often enough they can become 'truisms' all without qualifications or caveats."

Todd Hirsch, Senior Economist, ATB Financial

"Randy Park has once again hit the mark. All leaders should heed his warning and learn how to think and actually deal with the complex, ambiguous reality that confronts us. Come to think of it, everyone can benefit from this book to learn how to prepare for the future."

Shelle Rose Charvet, author, "Words That Change Minds"

What others said about "Thinking for Results":

"Randy Park has written a thoughtful and provocative book that will help broaden and deepen your thinking skills."

Mark Sanborn, author, "The Fred Factor: How Passion in Your Work and Life Can Turn the Ordinary into the Extraordinary"

"Useful tips and tools based on an easy to understand model of thinking. Everyone can use the book Thinking for Results."

Peter Urs Bender, author, "Leadership from Within"

"Thinking should produce results! That's just the first insight from Park's remarkable book. Since you are always thinking anyway, you might as well do it productively. No doubt about it - this book will get those mental wheels into high gear and help you go places!"

Ian Percy, author, "Going Deep"

"The concept of filters helps people to understand the frustrating puzzle of how a group of smart logical people can look at the same situation and come to very different conclusions. By examining one's filters one can often find previously overlooked solutions to simple, persistent, annoying problems."

Trevor Sparrow, Manager Process Consulting, Rogers Communications Customer Care

What others are saying about Randy Park:

"I truly was impressed with the participation and credit you for getting them involved from the start.... Everyone I have talked to was thankful for the opportunity to listen/participate and they were pleased that Finance took a step like this."
D. Culnan, Rogers Communications Inc.

"Randy Park has been our keynote and guest speaker on several occasions. His presentations have always been inspiring, informative and very worthwhile... Two-thumbs-up for Randy Park."
Wally Nickel, ISA Hamilton

"A lot of people were talking about your session for days afterwards. We use your language in our everyday discussions now. My colleagues just incorporate it into what they are saying and thinking. We will be discussing something and then, up pops the word 'filter.' That kind of impact on your day-to-day vocabulary, thinking, and communications is pretty dramatic."

Sheena August, Provincial Education Coordinator, Saskatchewan Housing Corporation

"As an association of members who share industry problems it was valuable to address some real-time issues. I heard many good remarks on the value of the tools you demonstrated."

Stephanie Reid, Membership Services Coordinator, Canadian Courier and Messenger Association

"We have regularly been hearing the word 'filters' in conversations in and about the office. Your talk has definitely opened up the minds of many and has had a lasting effect."

Mel Bahrey, Sales Associate, Willer Engineering Ltd.

"Wow Randy - you are an outstanding speaker. You are very interactive with good personal examples and really hold the audience's attention. Your slides are terrific and I enjoyed the way that you encouraged the participants to apply the information to their own jobs or lives."

Lynne Sinclair, Director of Education, Toronto Rehabilitation Institute

The Prediction Trap

and how to avoid it

Prosper Now and Prepare for the Future

Randy Park

*A*ronyd
*P*ublishing
Toronto, Canada

Published in 2008 by Aronyd Publishing, Toronto, Canada.

10 9 8 7 6 5 4 3 2 1

Library and Archives Canada Cataloguing in Publication

Park, Randy, 1956-
The prediction trap : (and how to avoid it!) / Randy Park.

Includes bibliographical references and index.
ISBN 978-0-9733926-1-6

1. Decision making. 2. Thought and thinking. 3. Forecasting.
I. Title.

BF441.P36 2008   153.8'3   C2008-904962-4

Visit Mr. Park's website at www.randypark.com

Printed and bound in Canada by Friesens

About the Author

Randy Park trained as a scientist and holds a Bachelor's degree in Physics and a Master's in Engineering Physics. From 1985 to 2000 he provided consulting, design, and training to dozens of world leading technology companies. While working with these organizations Randy observed that almost everyone, even the smartest people, have moments when they don't think very well.

Randy realized that many problems arise from a lack of understanding of our thinking processes. This was the impetus for the development of "Thinking for Results."

Randy is a Professional level member of the Canadian Association of Professional Speakers. In his keynote presentations and workshops, Randy stimulates his audiences to think more strategically by encouraging them to think about their thinking. From day to day decision making, problem solving, and communications to preparation for the long term, understanding how we think improves the decision making process.

Randy's first book *Thinking for Results – Success Strategies* was first printed in 2003 and is focused on thinking from an individual's point of view. In recent years his work has evolved to include enhancing group thinking and looking to the future. As you will see from this book, Randy believes that not enough attention is being paid to how we will work and live together in the future.

Randy is an accomplished sailor, having competed in sailing races (including two world championships) since he was twelve. He has also sailed from Hawaii to Vancouver, Canada. The use of strategy and effective thinking is crucial in sailing, and Randy draws on his sailing experience in his presentations and in his books. Randy now makes his home in Toronto, Canada.

To view articles, learn more about Randy, or engage him for your event, visit his web site at www.ThinkingforResults.com.

Acknowledgments

Once again, although I wrote this book there are many people to whom I am in debt for help along the way. In addition to the people I thanked in my first book, including my parents, this book is richer for the fact that I have met so many thoughtful people in the past three years.

For this book, my first and deepest thanks go to MIPG. The talented members — Beverly Beuermann-King, Shelle Rose Charvet, Ross Mackay, and Jean Sindon — are Canadian Association of Professional Speakers (CAPS) colleagues as well as true friends. They provided much helpful support, feedback, and prodding along the way.

Several people in Post Carbon Toronto have stimulated, challenged, and broadened my thinking, as well as providing valuable information and sources. This group of Toronto citizens works hard to educate people on energy issues. It is an amazing example of a group of very diverse people coming together with a common goal, and using that diversity constructively.

There are many other interesting and concerned people I have met in the past few months, some of whom provided comments on or are mentioned in this book. From business, academia, and the media, they provide me with optimism that some people besides me are looking at important, big picture issues.

Two others who have helped me along and deserve mention are Claire Sookman and Ursula Erasmus. Claire, you are a blast to work with, and our complementary styles always keep things interesting. Ursula, I thank you for your encouragement and our stimulating discussions.

As to other friends, I want to single out Sharon Martin. Our regular conversations are much appreciated — something I don't mention often enough.

In the actual production of the book, Cat Haggert is an excellent editor and proof reader who improved this book immensely, and thanks to Julie and Edgar at Walden Design for infusing the cover with life.

A special thank you to Friesen's printers from whom I won the first printing of the book at our CAPS convention. This book would not have happened — at least not when it did — if not for your generosity.

Finally, my wife Nora Cullen took over from her father in the "kept me going" department, regularly asking "is that book finished yet?" Thanks, Nora, for your patience, understanding, and love.

Randy Park

The
Prediction
Trap

and how to avoid it

Thinking for Results™

TABLE OF CONTENTS

Preface

This is a practical book about how people think and make decisions. From observing insightful inventions to watching brilliant people get stuck on simple little problems, I find the study of how and why people think the way they do to be fascinating. This book will not tell you how to think, or give you "seven secrets to successful thinking." Rather my hope is that it will both prompt you and help you to examine your own and others' thinking.

I'm concerned with what seems to be a decline in the quality of thinking these days. It could be that bad thinking is just more visible than good thinking; after all, the positive results that come from good decisions often don't have the same newsworthiness as the disasters that stem from bad thinking. Problems avoided are never as visible as problems that occur.

By bad thinking I mean decisions that are made with incomplete information or faulty logic. Sometimes this is accidental, sometimes it is deliberate, and sometimes bad thinking even pays off. Consider the corporate executives who make the front page of the newspaper because they make so many bad decisions that their companies pay them a carload of cash just to get rid of them. Bad strategic decisions by corporations, government boon-doggles, and stupid personal decisions (Google "the Darwin awards" for some humorous examples) appear to me to have one common thread — a lack of long-term, reality-based thinking.

Contrast that with organizations and governments that carefully assess the situation, think things through, and create plans for sustainable outcomes. If their approach also includes ongoing evaluation of the plans, incorporating new information when appropriate, then the chances are high they will create long-term value.

The speed of today's world in general and business in particular also affects thinking. The world moves ever faster and we live in the "just do it" society where getting any product out the door is often more important than getting a quality product out the door.

There are some exceptions to this short-term focus of many businesses. One recent development has been the rise of private capital buying out public corporations. Those behind the buyouts often assert that because they don't have the same concern for short-term share price they can take a longer-term view. (It will be interesting to see whether this is a net benefit for the economy and for society.)

In general, these days governments, businesses, and individuals are focused on the immediate, the here and now. Yet the biggest challenges we face worldwide require much longer-term thinking. The environment and climate change, energy supply and pricing, and global trade all require all of us to look beyond this quarter or next and look ahead a decade or more.

Over my lifetime, I have seen the nature of business change. It used to be that people invested in the shares of a business because they wanted to literally own a share of the business. The value of shares was based primarily on the value of the business — its assets and its ability to reliably generate revenue at that time and into the future. Now it seems that the value of a corporation's shares is based principally on what someone thinks somebody else will pay for the shares tomorrow. While this was certainly true in the past as well, these days it has become such a prominent factor that it skews the decision making of corporate executives. Time horizons have shrunk such that decisions are made principally based on the effect they will have on short-term share price. Since executive compensation is often based on share price, either directly through options or indirectly through other compensation, it reinforces this paradigm.

That thinking ahead is becoming less common in general should not come as a surprise. Look at the messages we are bombarded with and you will see two key themes. The first is instant gratification. The second is "what's in it for me?" Later in this book I will talk about "what's in it for me" and how self-interest is a core part of our thinking. The real problem occurs when instant gratification is coupled with a "what's in it for me" attitude. We end up with thinking that is often counterproductive to our individual or collective long-term interests. Too often today there is an intentional blindness to the reality of the physical world, the reality of people's differences, the reality of our own shortcomings in thinking, and the reality that we are all in this together. Albert Einstein's saying, "The significant problems we face can not be solved with the same level of thinking that created them," is no less true for having been quoted many times. Our world truly has become the "global village" of Marshall McLuhan. To deal effectively with the issues we face we must think better both individually and collectively. Yet many decisions I see being made come from less-enlightened thinking, not more; from shorter-term thinking, not longer.

There are some hopeful signs as well. In recent months as I have been working on this book I have met more and more people who are looking at long-term thinking; who are asking if the way we have structured our society and our businesses is working; and who are speaking out about the importance of the long view.

In the end, no matter how much wishing and hoping is done by adherents to the "law of attraction," economics, or a multitude of conflicting religions, reality will prevail. This is somewhat cold comfort to those of us who believe that the best way of dealing with a problem is to avoid it in the first place, but sometimes that too is reality. I imagine you are already considering these issues, otherwise you wouldn't have picked up this book. My hope is that my ideas will stimulate your own thinking and give you approaches to deal with others who don't think as well as you do.

Outline of the Book

Several years ago I began writing and speaking about how people think. My focus was (and still is) on how the decisions we make, both individually and collectively, influence the results we obtain. My early work and first book were about accurately perceiving current situations in the face of the influence of past experience and training — that is, how we make decisions in the present based on our past. But I realize now there was also a large aspect of the future involved in these decisions because we evaluate our current decisions based on the results we expect to obtain in the future.

Still, it wasn't until I started explicitly talking about anticipating the future that I realized the importance of this continuum between the past, present, and future with respect to how we think and make decisions. I say this because as I am assembling the chapters of this book I realize that it doesn't lend itself to a linear structure. This book is not so much traveling down a road as assembling a puzzle. To give you a sense of the overall picture, there are four major themes in this book: thinking accurately, understanding how other people think, effectively collaborating with others, and looking to the future.

The end goal of the book is to provide you with knowledge, insights, and approaches you can use to better deal with the future on an individual as well as collaborative basis. But in order to get there we need to put together some pieces of the puzzle that at first may seem quite disparate. I begin with a prologue discussing how most people look to the future, trying to predict what will happen. The next several chapters investigate our thinking processes as individuals, including a model of thinking and a look at thinking traps that can trip us up. In the next few chapters I expand the discussion of thinking to cover communicating with others and group thinking. Following that are several chapters on looking to the future, including both cautions and tips on how to do this. The last two chapters present a discussion of some important global issues and how they might affect your life.

Prologue

Our Fascination with the Future

"Who wants to know what their future will hold? Gaze into my crystal ball and the future will be revealed..." This is the way I begin some of my presentations, complete with a glowing crystal ball. Wouldn't it be nice to be able to predict the future? But I can't predict the future, fancy crystal ball or not. And neither can anyone else.

That doesn't stop us from trying. Think of how much of your life you spend thinking about things that might happen in the future. But if you think about it for ten seconds, you recognize that it is impossible to predict many important aspects of the future, there are too many variables and uncertainties. Of course, the focus of this book is on the future. I wrote this book because I think it is critically important that we plan for the future, especially in an increasingly resource-strained world. But I make a key distinction between predicting the future and anticipating the future. Part of the reason we like predictions is that our brains like absolutes — right or wrong, good or bad, something will or won't happen. We like absolutes because once we have labeled something with an absolute we figure we don't have to think about it anymore. I will address this idea of absolutes and extreme thinking in more detail later in the book.

Meanwhile, look at the number of leaders who developed a following simply because they expressed very strong convictions. In many cases they didn't actually do a good job or much for their followers. Especially in uncertain times, when people are afraid of what might happen, a leader who asserts that they know how things will unfold is appealing to many people. But in uncertain times I would argue that what you really want from a leader is someone who acknowledges the reality of the situation and wants to examine the alternatives and think things through, not someone who pig-headedly stays a course.

The media also prefers predictions to discussions of what "might" happen. Predictions make for nicer sound bites. And on radio or television it is much easier to present a single prediction than to even-handedly explore the subtle spectrum of an issue. In many cases, especially concerning politics, presenting one prediction can lead to a charge of bias. The media's common solution to this situation is to present two opposite predictions, and label it as balanced coverage. This can lead to some gamesmanship. If you are one of the two commentators and you know you are appearing at the same time as your opposition, you may be tempted to present your case a little more forcefully then you otherwise would. This again leads to the situation of polarized thinking and the framing of the situation as an either/or choice. This framing results in the loss of many of the subtleties of issues. It also implies that one viewpoint must be right and one wrong. It certainly doesn't lend itself to dialogue and compromise, but it is a rare situation when there aren't many points in between on the spectrum of the issue.

Of course, there are many fields such as science, engineering, and medicine that rely on proven experience as the basis of knowledge. In an organization, the advantage of sticking with the tried and true often means utilizing proven approaches that everyone knows how to execute. Many things will be the same tomorrow as they are today, which is why the Prediction Trap is so seductive.

Predicting the future is about creating and presenting one view of how the future will unfold. Anticipating and preparing for the future is about looking at multiple views of how the future might unfold. Even in the aforementioned fields of science, engineering, medicine, and law, good thinking includes considering the possibility that the current situation may be different from past experience.

In order to carry out the kind of anticipation I am talking about, our brains have to be able to hold multiple, possibly conflicting views of the future at one time. The way our brains have evolved makes this a challenging task. But the beauty of creating these different scenarios is that it opens up your thinking filter so that you may see information you had been missing. (If you haven't read my first book, thinking filters are a way of describing the automatic filtering of information your brain performs before you start consciously processing information. I will describe these filters in more detail in later chapters.) Later in this book I will also talk about some techniques you can use for yourself and your organization so that you can separate these different views to deal with them one at a time.

As an example, as a sailor, before I go on a trip I listen to the weather forecast as part of my preparations. But I certainly don't assume the forecast I hear will be right all the time; I want to be prepared for other eventualities as well.

One key to successfully developing these different views is to let go of the notion that you are trying to predict what is most likely to happen and view the process as simply creating stories about alternative futures. The number one reason for doing the work to anticipate the future, or multiple futures as I suggest, is that it is more likely to lead to long-term success. If it were possible to accurately predict the future and act accordingly you could take the course that leads to maximum success. But if you bet on just one prediction and it does not come true, the likelihood of wasted effort, poor results, and being blindsided by unexpected events skyrockets. Let's look at some of the factors that affect the success of a strategy or a product, and how they are affected by the two approaches — prediction of a single future versus anticipation of different futures.

Consider your stress level. If your plans are all based on a single view of the future, your stress will rise any time there is the slightest indication that things might not be turning out the way you expected. On the other hand, by anticipating different possibilities for the future, you can sleep well knowing things will be taken care of no matter what happens. The two different approaches will also have an effect on how you process information you receive. If you are predicting the future, you are invested in your guess. Your filtering of information will tend to be narrow; your filter will remain tuned to that one view of the future; and you will look for evidence to confirm your prediction. With the anticipation approach you are more flexible, with a more open filter to the information that you receive. In fact, you are more likely to actually seek out evidence that contradicts your current view of the world, meaning you are much less likely to be blindsided. If you are predicting the future you are also more likely to miss unexpected obstacles, when by anticipating the future you are more likely to notice them. But it is not all about minimizing risk. If you are predicting a single path to the future you are also more likely to miss unexpected opportunities, while the flexibility inherent in the anticipation process means you are more likely to notice them. And when the environment changes, as it often does, static predictions are threatened while dynamic anticipation is strengthened. In other words, prediction is based on perceived certainty and hope where anticipation is based on probability and realism.

FROM THE PAST TO THE PRESENT

CHAPTER 1

THE PAST–PRESENT–FUTURE CONTINUUM

I don't know about you, but when I stop to examine how I spend my time, a large proportion involves thinking about the past, planning for the future, reviewing actions I have taken, considering actions I might take, in short — living in times other than the present. Much of this book is about planning for the future, and an important part of that process is understanding your past. But I think it is very important to keep in mind that the only moment

in which you can act is the moment in front of you right now. Though this may seem obvious when you think about it, it's important to be consciously aware of this continuum when you are making decisions. What you have experienced in your past has had a substantial impact on how you will make decisions today. What you imagine for the future will also mold your thought processes. Try this thought experiment to illustrate my point. Imagine you have created in your mind a new device to transport people. This device is unlike anything that currently exists. And yet even to have that picture in your own head you must relate it to something from your past. You might use a description to yourself such as "it is like a miniature car" or "it is like a moving sidewalk" or even "it is like the teleporter on *Star Trek*." And if you want to communicate your idea to someone else, once again the words that you use, the analogies you draw, will be based on past experiences you and the other person have in common. How would you describe an airplane to someone who had never seen one? You would probably call it a mechanical bird. This approach is evident in some of the names we end up using for these inventions, for example "moving sidewalk" (which to someone who had never seen one might sound quite absurd!) Experts in a field can get caught up in their past in a way that limits their creativity. I've seen this in both myself and in others. Someone might propose an idea for a new product, and the "experts," those with the most experience, will start relating the idea to their past experience and knowledge and determining if it will work. In the worst case this can come across as a negative, "that will never work" attitude. Certainly realism in implementation is a crucial step in product design, but sometimes injecting this type of realism too early in the creative process restricts ideas. Besides, I have seldom seen product creation come about as a simple straight line from A to B. In most cases, there are different avenues explored, dead ends reached, backtracking, and reassessment of ideas. Letting the past in the form of experience limit which roads are explored can block a path which might not lead directly to the final product but does so indirectly. I don't think I can overemphasize the influence your past has on your future thinking. Our pasts are like the air we breathe — we are so immersed in them that we seldom consciously think about their importance.

How often have you heard someone say (or said yourself), "I tried that once before, and it didn't work." Or alternatively, "Well, I did it that way before and it worked." Over-reliance on the past creates a type of bias. Fortunately, in science we have a rigorous process that scientists follow precisely to reduce this bias. Otherwise, for example, we might have unproven and unsafe drugs on the market at the same time as we'd miss out on drugs that didn't work for one scientist but might have worked for thousands of other people. While trying something only once does make sense in some situations (especially life threatening ones!) there are many examples where a sample of one is not adequate to draw any general conclusions.

What about the other end of the time line, the future? I do think it is extremely important to anticipate and plan for the future. After all, 24 hours from now tomorrow will be your present and the future time period you have been contemplating (though not necessarily the events) will happen. But I believe it is important to remember that there is no guarantee that the future will unfold the way you expect. The most obvious example in recent memory is September 10, 2001. An extremely small number of people in the world expected the events of September 11 to happen.

We cannot directly control the future, any more than we can predict it. But in the same way that we anticipate the future, we can steer the future in the direction we plan through our actions. As is the case with steering a ship, we sometimes have to correct our course. And wind, waves, and currents may push us off the course we had planned. Nevertheless, without the plan, and the action of steering, we are drifting rudderless on the sea. Even when we steer into the future we rely on our past experiences and training in knowing which direction to push the wheel. As conditions change we need to be prepared to adjust our approach and be prepared for situations that are significantly different from our past experience. We can't predict with certainty whether a storm will arrive on our trip. But we can prepare for the storm, just as we can prepare for excellent weather. If we do that then we are ready and able to capitalize on new situations as they arrive, so that we not only notice a new, favorable wind, but are able to take advantage of it.

Both those who plan and those who don't plan sometimes lose sight of the fact that we only act in the present. We cannot act in the past, and though we can learn from it, we cannot live in it. We cannot act in the future, and though we should prepare for it, we cannot live in it. While too little planning can lead to disaster, too much planning and not enough action in the present can lead to solid ideas but no tangible results. I ought to know; I sometimes fall into that trap myself.

CHAPTER 2

YOUR PAST AND HOW YOU THINK

The next three chapters will be familiar to you if you've read my first book *Thinking for Results — Success Strategies*. These chapters describe the Thinking for Results model that forms the basis for both my previous book and this one. It's no secret that despite our living in the information age, the key to better thinking is not more information. The Internet (and especially spam) illustrate that more information does not necessarily make us smarter, it is what we do with information that is key.

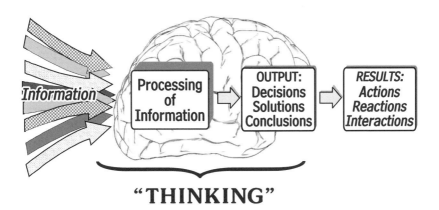

A practical definition of thinking is to "take in information, process it, and reach some conclusions, decisions, or solutions." From the conclusions, we usually take some actions — work, play, communicate — that lead to the results we create in our lives. Sometimes our thinking leads us to the decision to not take any action. This will also lead to some results. The figure shows this process. All of the results that show up in our lives, both the ones we like and the ones we don't like, are consequences of our thinking. Even when events occur that are outside of our realm of control (such as the weather), our reaction to these events or our actions prior to the events — in other words, our thinking — will determine our results.

(You might have heard of *The Secret* movie and book. Since I wrote *Thinking for Results — Success Strategies* these have received quite widespread publicity. I now find it important to point out that while I say our thinking determines our results I don't mean it in the sense that *The Secret* does. They claim "It is exactly like placing an order from a catalog... You must know that what you want is yours the moment you ask." and "See yourself living in abundance and you will attract it. It works every time, with every person." I'll talk more about *The Secret* in a later chapter.)

I certainly believe that attitude is important, but so is the thinking prior to the events, for example our preparedness. An attitude of "we'll make it through no matter what" is certainly helpful in climbing a mountain. But without proper preparation and equipment no amount of attitude will get you to the top. A late colleague of mine, Peter Urs Bender, was known for saying "Your past was perfect to get you where you are today. This does not mean you had a perfect past..." You are where you are today, and you will be where you will be tomorrow, as a result of your analysis of the circumstances and stimuli you face. And while your past was perfect to get you where you are today, this does not mean it is perfect to get you to where you want to go tomorrow. If you improve the quality of your thinking you are more likely to achieve the results that you seek and less likely to achieve undesired results.

I trained as a scientist, and many of my colleagues and clients are people with scientific or technical training. I have observed that people in these fields (myself included) believe that they are logical thinkers. Accountants, lawyers, politicians, doctors, and many others tell us they look at "just the facts."

I would agree that in the vast majority of cases these people, and most others, process information logically, rationally, and consistently. If they are all processing the same information they will all arrive at the same conclusions. So why are there so many different conclusions from these people? We ask doctors for "a second opinion." We have lawyers passionately arguing both sides of a case. In accounting there can be different ways of viewing corporate finance. Even in science there is sometimes disagreement. As for politicians, it is almost impossible to find a politician who isn't convinced that their way is the right way. Yet all these groups have rational, logical arguments supporting their point of view. How can this be? It's because the simple model shown in the previous figure has a key piece missing: our "filters." The next figure shows a much more accurate picture of how we think. The

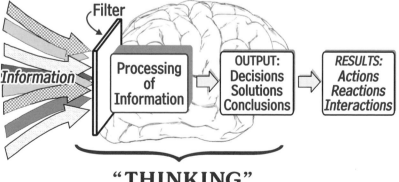

key difference is the addition of a filter in the thinking process that filters the information before it reaches the processing part of our brains. The analogy I use for these filters is colored plastic or glass that filters light. The bookmark you may have received with this book has a color picture of this Model of Thinking. You can also see examples of filters on the Thinking for Results website at www.ThinkingforResults.com. If you have some old 3-D glasses or other red or blue filters, pull them out and try looking at the model first through the red filter and then through the blue filter. (In my keynote presentations and workshops I hand out colored plastic filters for participants. If you would like your own red and blue filters or need a bookmark, call, write, or e-mail us and we will happily mail you a set.)

When you look at the colored Model of Thinking on the bookmark, you can see that different sources of information are colored differently. If we view information without the filters, we see it all. But when we view information through our personal filters — red or blue in this example — some of the information is blocked or changed. The information that reaches the processing part of our thinking depends on the characteristics of our filters. The nature of these filters and everyday examples are explored in much greater depth in my book *Thinking for Results — Success Strategies*. Our thinking filters are made up of our assumptions, our beliefs, and our biases — filters that modify the incoming information, often without our being aware of them doing so.

If you look at the model through the plastic filters or 3-D glasses, you are holding these filters in your hand, so you are very aware that you are looking through a filter. In the case of our thinking filters, it is more like wearing sunglasses — we put them on and then often forget we are wearing them — yet they still filter what we perceive and process. The filters in our brains are not just "blue" or "red" but are much more complex than that. In general your filter will be different from my filter, which will be different from someone else's filter. Thus even when we're standing at the same place, observing the same situation at the same time, our different filters mean that we will process different information. Although we may use the same (logical) processing in analyzing the situation, we are looking at different filtered information. Thus our conclusions will likely be different. This analogy is similar to the expression "looking at the world through rose-colored glasses" referring to someone who is filtering out bad news. (The expression implies a kind of naivety, which can sometimes be the effect of our filters.) Sometimes your filter hinders your thinking by blocking important information. On the other hand, your filter can be very useful. In everyday life it filters out extraneous information — when you're walking down the street for example. Think of the information overload if you had to consciously analyze every advertisement, store display, street sign, person, and vehicle that you saw and heard!

In the tasks you are good at your filter forms a large part of your expertise. Your filter allows you to do things like pattern recognition — recognizing, identifying, and analyzing situations very quickly. You couldn't carry out many of your normal functions — such as driving a car — if it weren't for your automatic processing of pieces of information by your filter.

One way to significantly improve your thinking comes from the old saying "two heads are better than one." When you incorporate someone else's knowledge and experience, their filter, into your thinking you can often find better solutions more quickly. You don't have to agree with them; you don't even have to incorporate their perspective if you decide not to. But I have found that looking at my position using the benefit of someone else's filter helps me better understand my own viewpoint and filter.

There is much more on utilizing other people's filters in subsequent chapters.

I'll wrap up this chapter by recapping some properties of our filters. Our filters consist of many things: our beliefs, our habits, our assumptions, our knowledge, our attitudes, our prejudices, our training, our opinions, our experiences. They are the sum total of our past learning, our past thinking, our past actions, and our past experiences.

Consider how your filter influences your thinking — for example, the beliefs you have or assumptions you might make. It could be that for "politicians" you have a filter that "politicians are well intentioned, honorable people; politicians work very hard." Or maybe your filter is "politicians are self-centered, power-hungry people; politicians only care about themselves."

Can you see how your filter is going to affect the decisions and conclusions you reach? If your filter for politicians is that they are honest, hard working, and dedicated you are less likely to let through information suggesting political scandal. If your filter for the economy is that it is a disaster, you will process information that suggests things are going badly and block information suggesting things will improve. Other examples where people often have strong filters are business leaders, the economy, globalization, charity, and the environment. Think for a minute now about the characteristics of your filter in these areas.

Thinking is more than just processing using logic and rules. The biggest challenges we face in our jobs, our relationships, our organizations, and our world for that matter, are the ones where our assumptions filter our information, influence our thinking, and affect our results.

Chapter 3

Feedback Along the Way

Life teaches us lessons. Some lessons we are quick to learn; some lessons take longer. Sometimes life has to keep hitting us over the head with a large stick before we get it. How quickly we learn these lessons depends to a great extent on how we process the information we receive from the results we create. Thus a key component to add to our thinking model is feedback.

The word feedback is now commonly used in a context such as "Can I give you some feedback?" which seems to me to often mean some sort of criticism. But in technology feedback has a very specific meaning. Feedback is taking a measurement of the output and including it as an input to control the process. A simple example would be bottles moving along an assembly line, which you are filling with juice. By monitoring the level of the juice in each bottle as it is being filled you could stop filling at the appropriate time. This is the conventional, technical definition of feedback. When it comes to Thinking for Results, feedback helps us judge if we are on course to reach our objectives, or if we need to adjust our actions by changing our thinking. The feedback that originates from our results can be provided by our colleagues, our boss, our spouse, our children. For an organization, feedback can come from customers or suppliers. To use the feedback we look at our desired results and compare them to the results we are achieving, as indicated by the feedback. If they match, we continue our current thinking. If they don't match, then we have to change our thinking and our actions if we truly want to achieve the results we say we want. Of course, most people use feedback daily, either consciously or without thinking about it.

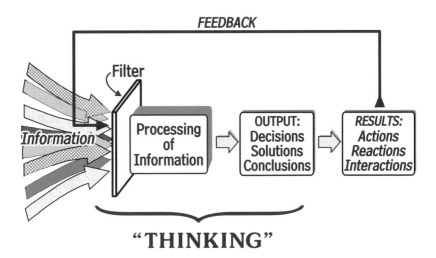

So how does feedback fit into our model of thinking? If we look at the expanded model shown in the figure above we see that the feedback information travels from our results back to form part of the input into our thinking process. The key aspect of this feedback is that the feedback goes back to our filters. Think about this for a minute — in fact, think of a personal example, a situation where you had an idea or opinion you strongly believed in. What did you do if you ran into information that suggested your idea or opinion might have shortcomings? If you are like most people, you did not place as much stock in that information as you did in information that supported your position.

A common example is people's opinions of the stock market.

Whether the market is going up or down, whether they own stocks or not, people's filters significantly affect what feedback is transmitted through to the logical processing part of their thinking. Thus we have to make an extra effort to understand and identify our filters so we can effectively utilize feedback, whether it is feedback we observe ourselves or feedback that is provided by others. If you filter out the feedback before it reaches your processing, it is obviously of no use. The value of feedback to your thinking process is proportional to the amount of feedback that passes through your filter.

How often have you had someone ask you for feedback on an idea, then, when you tried to provide it you were met with "No, you don't understand, I've already taken care of that." A number of years ago I was in a group doing presentation rehearsals. We would each present a 10-minute segment, and then get feedback on the presentation. The rule in the group was the only thing you could say in response to the feedback was "Thank you." The reason for the rule was that if someone is receiving feedback but thinking about how to respond to the feedback — often defensively — they won't hear the feedback accurately and gain the most benefit from it. Their filter will likely block much useful information.

It is important to pay attention to the feedback we receive, whether it is from our own observations or from others. Unless we have done something many times, it is likely that the feedback will suggest we need at least minor adjustments to reach our desired results. That is to be expected. The Thinking for Results approach is to use the feedback to fine-tune our thinking. Not Thinking for Results would be to ignore the feedback and hang on to our original thinking.

Personally, I don't buy the maxim "There are no mistakes, only learning experiences." Some things are clearly mistakes — like if someone assembling equipment installs a part backwards. Just don't compound the mistake by ignoring it — make the effort to ensure that it is a learning experience. Find the reason the mistake was made — was it improper process, poor training, sloppiness? Then utilize the feedback to reduce the likelihood of it happening again.

You likely already do this monitoring and fine tuning of your results in some areas of your life. What I'm encouraging you to do is be more aware of how you do it. If you play any sports or games, think about your favorite activity. (If you don't play any sports or games, think of a moderately complicated task at work that you do repeatedly.) Now think of the types of feedback you receive when doing this activity. Consider the different sources for the feedback you have identified. For example, if your activity is golf, your feedback would probably come from your score, your partner, your instructor if you use one, and maybe the people playing behind you if you're really slow. Other sources of feedback in general can include the time it takes to complete a task, costs, customer feedback, performance evaluations, etc.

Now consider the weight you put on feedback in general. When you receive feedback do you take it into consideration or do you filter it out? Remember that any information must pass through your filter before you can consciously process it. Feedback that is blocked by your filter provides no new input to your processing.

Consider two possibilities: the feedback supports your current actions, or the feedback suggests you need to alter your actions to reach your desired results. As objectively as you can, rate yourself on the following scales:

Feedback that supports my actions:

I consider it — — — — — — — I ignore it

Feedback that suggests I need to change my actions:

I consider it — — — — — — — I ignore it

Is there a difference? Remember that one definition of insanity is doing the same thing over and over but expecting different results. Our filters can be so strong that they block out feedback that doesn't fit our preconceived picture of how things should be.

Finally, consider how much emphasis you put on feedback based on its source. In the sports example, do you place more emphasis on feedback from your instructor? You probably do, and that makes sense, they are the pro. But do you ignore feedback from other sources? Maybe your golf partner sees you doing the same thing over and over and points it out to you. Do you listen? (Does it make a difference if your partner is also your spouse?) Note that whether you listen or not will depend in large part on your filter about the source — how do you judge their expertise? What about your score — if you have a bad game, do you examine what happened or explain it away based on being distracted, or tired, or bad weather? Think of some examples where you receive feedback, and how open you are to it based on how much credibility you give the feedback.

As I said earlier, we are always receiving feedback. Next to being very clear about the results we seek, feedback is probably the most useful tool we have in improving our thinking to reach the results we say we want. To fully benefit from the feedback we must sometimes make extra effort to ensure the feedback is not blocked by our filters. Thus it is extremely important to understand how our filters affect this feedback if we want to maximize its benefits. The amount of openness you have to a piece of feedback is reflected in your filters. Don't forget that you can consider feedback without necessarily agreeing with it. My favorite saying is from Aristotle: "It is the mark of an educated mind to be able to entertain a thought without accepting it." You can let the feedback through your filter and process it without accepting that it is true for you or true in general. In fact, I believe this is one of the keys to progress in our organizations and in our world — the ability to open our filters to see others' points of view.

Chapter 4

Then What Happens?

(The Gedanken Step)

In the last chapter we looked at the feedback we receive from the world regarding the actions (or inactions) we take in response to our thinking. This feedback is one way that we can determine if we are on course, if we are achieving the results we desire. But what about those times when you might have said to yourself "Why did I do that?" Or when you don't have the time or resources to try something and wait for feedback? How can we improve the Thinking for Results model and process to reduce the number of times that we say, "I wish I hadn't done that!"? In this chapter I am going to add one last step to the Thinking for Results model. This step is called the Gedanken step, or "Then What Happens?"

Gedanken is a German word popularized (okay, popularized amongst physicists) by Albert Einstein. Gedanken means "thought experiment." The purpose of this step is to do a "thought experiment," anticipate what will happen, and feed back the anticipated results into our thinking process before we actually take action. By taking our original conclusions or decisions and giving them a second thought, feeding them back and looking at them again, we can often avoid mistakes, save time or money, or discover a better way of doing things. Let me add a caution at this point. The purpose in Thinking for Results is "a little more thinking for a lot better results." It is possible to do too much thinking such that you spend all your time thinking and no time doing. (I sometimes get caught in this "analysis paralysis" myself.) How do you know if this is happening? Take a look at your results — if you are not getting any results, either desired or undesired, you are probably not taking enough action.

The idea of taking a second look at our decisions before carrying them out is not a new idea. In fact, I would argue that in decades past, people were more likely to examine their thinking than they are today. There could be many reasons for this — one reason is that people are asked today to make more decisions in less time and with fewer resources. But I also believe that Western society has a growing tendency to leap before we look. One reason I believe this has developed is because fewer and fewer of us work with physical objects in our jobs. In years past, more people were involved in constructing physical items, where it is important to get it right the first time. For example, people who build a bridge have to plan carefully, do the calculations and think things through. The consequences of not getting it right the first time are large. But in the case of information, documents and reports can be easily edited and modified. I believe that this has contributed to the "get it done as fast as possible" type of attitude, which I find much more prevalent than it used to be. Our leisure activities have changed as well. Years ago, men might have a workshop and women might sew. When building something, it is important to remember the old adage, measure twice, cut once. Similarly in sewing, there is no "undo" button if you cut the material too short. Nowadays, much of our leisure time is spent surfing the

Internet, where we always have a back button, or playing computer games where the consequences of being "killed" are small. The games themselves are also largely about reaction time and making quick moves and decisions. Compare that to chess, which teaches the players to think in advance, look at possible moves, anticipate the other player's actions, and weigh the different consequences.

The risk in rushing the creation of a document may not be as serious as the type of risk that we face with a poorly designed bridge. But the costs can still be significant. For example, I might prepare a report for my boss or a client with the attitude that I will get it done as quickly as possible and polish up the details later. My justification might be that "they always have comments or changes anyway, why bother spending time on precise wording, or grammar and spelling." But there are at least two consequences to this approach. First of all, I might present myself to my boss or client as someone who does sloppy work. Second of all, I waste some of everyone's time because even if my ideas are good, I will have to edit and present a second polished version. In addition, if the draft version is poorly crafted, my intended meaning may not be clear. Finally, I'm wasting my own time generating two versions of the same document. It reminds me of another saying, "If you don't have time to do it right, when will you have time to do it over?" Similar results occur if your work is part of a larger process — and these days this is true for most people. If you are part of a team writing computer software for example, if your section has bugs in it and you pass it on to someone else, they may spend hours trying to figure out why the system doesn't work. A little extra thinking and checking on your work and you might have located the bug in your section in five minutes. To turn the tables, how do you feel when this happens to you?

In the 1980s, when Tom Peters wrote *In Search of Excellence* one of his mantras was "Ready, Fire, Aim." In his opinion, at that time organizations had become too rigid, too bureaucratic, too bloated. Managers in these organizations spent much of their time sitting around thinking, trying to perfect their decisions, and never actually taking any action. These days I think the opposite is true.

So what exactly is this Gedanken or Then What Happens? step? As shown in the figure, after you reach your conclusions and your decisions, you feed those results of your thinking process back in to the input of your thinking. Once again, as with the external feedback, the information passes through your filter. If you're not aware of how your filter modifies the information you are considering, you may still have blind spots. The usefulness of this internal feedback step, as with the external feedback, is dependent on you understanding your filter.

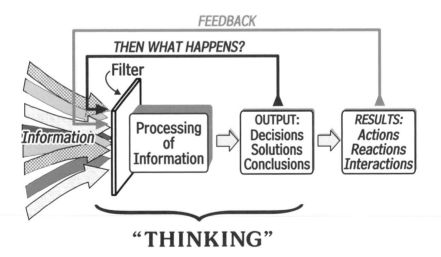

What is the cost in doing this extra thinking? In many cases, it is simply a few extra seconds of time to review the information and decide if acting on these conclusions will yield the results you want. If you are sure, then go ahead. If not, then why not take a little more time to review your decision? Then What Happens? doesn't mean doing everything twice. In fact it is somewhat ironic that the more you use the Then What Happens? step, the better your thinking becomes and the less you have to do things twice. Another area where the Then What Happens? step can be very useful is when communicating with other people. Stopping and thinking Then What Happens? before saying something can spare you a lot of negative feedback. Whether you are writing a letter, creating a report, doing an experiment, talking to someone, or any other task you carry out, in my experience it is rare that a few extra seconds of thinking won't pay for themselves.

The basic Thinking for Results model is now complete. Putting this into practice can be summed up in three steps:

1. Check your filter

2. Think it through

3. Then what happens?

Most of the emphasis in *Thinking for Results — Success Strategies* was on recognizing and understanding your filters. In this book the emphasis is on the second and third steps — processing the information, then looking to the future, from the personal to the global context, and asking "Then what happens?"

Chapter 5

Using Intuition and Trusting Your Gut

Let's look at some of the details of how this idea of filtering manifests itself in day-to-day thinking. I described earlier how our filters affect the results of our thinking by limiting or modifying the information that reaches the conscious, thinking part of our brains. It is important to understand this mechanism not just because it happens automatically, but also because it happens so quickly. A demonstration that I use in my presentations is to flash a picture on the screen for a fraction of a second and ask people if they recognize any objects. This picture is reproduced on the next page. Try this exercise now by flipping quickly to the next page and back to this page. When you do this, take a glance at the picture, and then flip the page back. After you have done that, see if you recall recognizing any images. I typically flash the picture twice, and most people in the audience tell me that they do recognize an object — a cat. (Out west, some people see a cowboy boot or an antler. People with even wilder imaginations have come up with other objects as well.) What happens in this exercise is that the filter in your brain matches the shapes it sees in the fraction of a second with a mental database of shapes you have seen in the past. In the fraction of the second that you see this image, you don't have time to consciously analyze all of the shapes to determine if you recognize any of them. But your filter operates at a much faster time scale than your conscious processing.

Malcolm Gladwell wrote the bestseller, *Blink*, describing many situations where this filtering and pattern matching occurs. He provides some interesting examples of experts who used their intuition or gut feeling — basically their filters — to analyze situations and reach conclusions.

There is no doubt that this level of expertise is helpful in many situations. On the other hand, if you are not aware that you are using your filter in this way, and reach conclusions based on your past experiences, you can get stuck down a blind alley. And because this intuition or gut feeling analysis occurs so quickly it can be easy to miss its importance. I see people, myself included, spend significant amounts of time on a conscious, logical analysis of a problem or strategy that is based on an assumption that was made in a fraction of a second. Sometimes that assumption is totally inaccurate, and negates the value of all the time spent analyzing the issue.

Being aware of your filters is about keeping an open mind, but it is about even more than that. It's about an awareness that your mind can close in a fraction of a second because of an unrecognized trigger between the present and your past experiences. Just like the picture of the cat, your brain latches on to the familiar. In fact, many people tell me that when I flash the picture with the cat a second time, they focus more intently on the cat to confirm what they had seen the first time. Thus they are less likely, not more, to see new shapes the second time around.

A couple of years ago, I almost missed out on a good idea from a student after I gave a guest lecture at a prominent business school. She came up to me after my presentation and said "I have a great idea for your next book." Instantly my filter popped up. I don't want to write another book right now! Consider the situation —

I had just completed a 45-minute talk on filters, I write about filters all the time, and still it was all I could do to recognize and suspend my own filter, and listen and really hear her idea. It turns out her idea could be really good for a companion workbook that I had thought about writing but hadn't started because I didn't have the core idea I needed. But if I'd gone with my first filter, and just stood there and nodded politely, I never would have heard her idea.

For a little while one of the popular topics for management books was the idea of intuition and trusting your gut. Business leaders such as Jack Welch talked about using their intuition in their decision making. In my mind there are two important questions that come from that type of statement: How does their gut know what to do? and Can other people be taught this skill?

A lot of my personal experience with trusting my gut or intuition comes from sailing situations. I have raced sailboats most of my life and at various times have been quite successful. In sailboat racing some things are essential to be competitive — a good boat, physical skill, knowledge of the rules, and a good understanding of the principles of sailing. But the key to winning a sailboat race is the tactics involved. There is a lot of information to analyze in a sailboat race. Some of this information, such as the general weather trends and the abilities of other competitors, can be known and analyzed ahead of time. This allows the racer to filter out some information in advance. For example, if I know that a particular boat typically doesn't do very well, I'm not likely to pay much attention to it during the race (though this can be a mistake at times.) Other information changes within seconds while you are on the course, necessitating quick processing of information.

Sometimes decisions can be thought through logically using the Thinking for Results model — being aware of your filters, looking at the feedback, thinking Then What Happens? But there are many variables in the race and often decisions must be made in fractions of a second, leaving no time for a thorough analysis. This is when intuition, or trusting your gut, comes into play. Although top sailors are very thorough in their analysis of some aspects of the race, there are also many times when they trust their guts. If you ask the top sailors why they changed course at a particular point in a race, often their answer will simply be "it felt like the right thing to do." Of course, this can confuse amateur sailors who then try to sail according to what feels right. The key difference is that the expert sailor has built up an accumulated database from thinking the situations through consciously. Without the conscious analysis of successes and mistakes, the "gut" — which is really their filter — has nothing to compare to. Essentially the novice has an open or inaccurate filter, whereas the expert has a finely tuned filter.

The Achilles' heel of the expert is when a situation arises that is different from one they have encountered in the past. In sailing, an unknown competitor, the wind blowing from a different direction than usual, or an unfamiliar boat can put the expert at a severe disadvantage because the filter that is usually such an asset can end up blocking out important information.

This observation about gut feeling has extremely important applications in business. I have seen individuals, companies, and industries with finally tuned filters that allow them to quickly make the best decisions in their business — as long as there are no major changes or discontinuities between the present and the past. But they can be blind to the point of making ridiculous decisions if an unexpected situation comes along. One way to guard against this happening to you is to be sure you associate with people outside of your own company and industry. There is more on the topic of "trusting your gut" and the related topic of "parallel processing" in my first book *Thinking for Results — Success Strategies*.

Given the importance of your filter to your thinking process, an obvious question is does your filter change over time? And can you change your own filter? It depends on what part of your filter you are considering. Some aspects of your filter are fairly easy to change, some are harder, and some cannot be changed. The best way to understand this is to look at the next figure. This shows a hierarchy of thinking with some general labels and descriptions. Note that this is a general guide; there are no hard and fast divisions between these different levels. Beginning at the top there is the level of logic. This is the processing part of conscious thinking. People make observations (of their filtered information) and logically analyze the information to reach conclusions. The next level down is also part of conscious thinking, but is carried out

Thinking Hierarchy

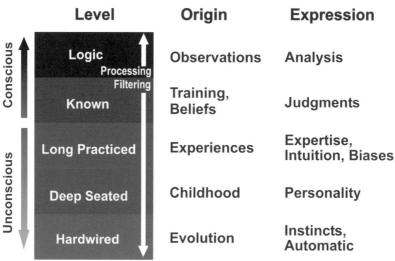

Level	Origin	Expression
Logic *Processing Filtering*	Observations	Analysis
Known	Training, Beliefs	Judgments
Long Practiced	Experiences	Expertise, Intuition, Biases
Deep Seated	Childhood	Personality
Hardwired	Evolution	Instincts, Automatic

primarily by filtering functions. These are the filters we know about, our expertise that has been developed through training for example. These are also beliefs, values, and morals. As a result their expression is usually in the form of judgments, either professional judgments or value judgments. If someone asks us about these filters we can easily explain what they are and how they developed. Going deeper into the thinking continuum we reach the below-conscious thinking and filtering that occurs.

The highest level of unconscious filtering is long-practiced habits and assumptions. Primarily these come from life experiences and are reinforced by the feedback received in life. Some of our expertise and skills, and our intuition or gut feelings are in this level. Our biases and prejudices also tend to be long-practiced filters. This is a level we are not normally aware of but can bring into consciousness by observing the decisions we make. Moving still further down the hierarchy we reach the deep-seated filters that most likely were developed during childhood and adolescence. This type of filter is usually expressed as parts of our personality. Finally, at the lowest level are the hardwired, instinctive aspects of thinking. These are the automatic reactions that developed through genetic evolution as a species. Our genes also have a large influence on our personality through the characteristics passed down from our parents.

When you look at this hierarchy there are a couple of trends that become apparent. One is that the higher levels in this hierarchy are both easier to observe and easier to change. In Thinking for Results and in understanding the effect that our thinking process has on our decisions, we are primarily looking at the filters in the known and the long-practiced areas of this hierarchy. These are the ones that we can either observe directly, simply by stopping and thinking about it, or indirectly by looking at the decisions we make given different types of input information. These are also filters that can be changed if we choose to change them. Some take more work than others, but it is possible to alter them through awareness and practice. In contrast, the thinking governed by some of the hardwired characteristics of our brains cannot be changed.

Another observation is that there is a natural progression that occurs from the higher levels of this hierarchy to the lower levels when we see the same information or make the same decisions multiple times. One of the principal reasons for practicing a sport or an act is to take the thinking involved from the conscious, logical processing level down through the known and filtering into the long-practiced, unconscious filtering — the level of unconscious competence. One reason to move these skills from the higher levels of thinking to the lower levels is because the lower levels have faster reaction times. Conscious, logical processing takes the most amount of time, filtering takes less time, and the hardwired responses are the fastest. In many situations — sports and musical performance are obvious examples — being able to perform quickly is a key to success.

There is also more emotion involved with the lower levels of thinking. This can lead to hazardous situations, where we react quickly, "without thinking," with an emotional response. The expression "pushing someone's buttons" accurately describes this type of situation — the quick production of an often illogical response from an emotional trigger. Another thing that psychological studies have proven is that the more our brains are stressed, the further down the hierarchy we go and the more automatic our reactions tend to be. This is valuable to realize because what it tells you is that when you are in a situation of stress you are more likely to fall back on your filters. If the situation is a familiar one, relying on your filters is an effective tactic. But if the situation is not a familiar one, your filters may block important information that is right in front of you.

Chapter 6

Potholes in Present-Tense Perception

There are several common traps that people fall into when analyzing information and making decisions. Sometimes they arise
because of our filters; other times they are more like flaws in
logic, though in many cases they are some of both. There are
several very good references on thinking traps that I have listed in
the bibliography. In this chapter I want to give an overview of
some of these traps and their common manifestations. I'll start
with the traps that are most closely related to the way our brains
process information. The first two traps occur because of the
limited ability of our brains to consider several pieces of information at once. If I read you a long list of three digit numbers, once
I reached somewhere around the 10th number you would likely
have trouble recalling some of the earlier numbers from the list,
though you could probably remember the last few numbers. (You
can try this with the list of numbers on the next page; move your
hand or a piece of paper down the list to cover up the numbers as
you read them.)

Of course if any of the numbers had particular significance to
you, they would be much easier to remember. For example, if an
address at which you had lived was among the numbers, you
would likely remember that it was one of the numbers. In addition, you will likely recall that the number 911 is one of the

```
848
223
247
236
815
203
740
842
596
911
417
963
767
280
173
226
926
137
855
845
618
182
```

numbers, either because of associating it with the emergency number or with the events of September 11. This exercise illustrates the foundations of two thinking traps. One is that we more easily recall recent information and therefore tend to put disproportionate emphasis on this information — the recency thinking trap. Another thinking trap, which is really a manifestation of our filters, is the familiarity trap — if a piece of information seems familiar, it more easily passes our filter and therefore receives more weight. The example in the number list is 911.

The recency trap can be especially distorting when coupled with the way that media typically report information. They are called the "news" media for a reason — they are supposed to present new information. However, the result is that when a reader or listener of the news receives a report, they are often only getting the new information and not important background information or information that had been reported earlier. If the story is one that the news consumer has been following, where they have a good understanding of the issue, this would not be a problem. But if it is an issue that they are unfamiliar with or only encounter infrequently, they may have forgotten the background of the story. They may reach a conclusion based almost solely on the recent information.

A "we've heard that before" response is a common one even for important issues if they have been known for a while. Since the news media is focused on what is new, consistency of principles or obviousness of an argument are generally uninteresting. A politician who has lobbied all their career for education programs for underprivileged children will not likely achieve as much publicity as someone who makes an outrageous statement such as "they must have done something to attract their misfortune." A Green Party candidate's position on the environment is not going to be as newsworthy as a Conservative Party announcement, because most people know (or think they know) what the Green Party candidate will say. But the truth doesn't become less true or less important with age or retelling. It just becomes less newsworthy and thus less reported.

Consider another thinking trap that is commonly exploited by retailers. Are you attracted by a sale? When deciding on a product, is your thinking swayed by the difference between a regular price and a sale price? If so, you may be vulnerable to the anchoring trap. The anchoring trap is where disproportionate weight is given to the first information we receive. Advertisers and retailers display a "regular price" to anchor a value for the product in your head. By then offering a "sale price" it appears you are receiving a bargain. It sets your filter for a certain price. In my experience, in the last few years retailers have used this technique so often that many consumers will not buy anything at the so-called regular price anymore. In fact, consumers now expect that everything will go on sale at one point or another. Let me provide another example of the anchoring trap. What are your answers to the following two questions: 1. Is the distance to the moon greater or less than 100 million miles? 2. What is your best guess of the distance from the earth to the moon? If you're like most people, then unless you already had an idea of the distance to the moon, the 100 million mile figure influenced your answer to the second question. Studies in groups have shown that those who were supplied with a larger number for the first question tended to guess a larger number in the second question.

Now for an example of the thinking trap that commonly shows up with investments and the stock market. Most people like to be right in any decision they make. Consequently, after making a decision they find it more difficult to change their mind and reverse the decision. In the first place it would mean admitting that their first decision wasn't the best one. In the second place, reversing the decision is making another decision meaning another opportunity to make a mistake. Thus people have a tendency to stick with the status quo. In investments (and I have done this myself) they will hang on to a stock even as it continues to decline in value rather than objectively looking at the information and making a decision to sell. In business, choosing the status quo over other options often is seen as a less risky course because "this is the way we've always done it," and who can be faulted for sticking with the tried and true? And it is often true that the status quo is the best course of action. The status quo thinking trap is the failure to reevaluate the decision on a regular basis. Once this thinking trap is operating, the filters perpetuate the status quo by passing supporting information and blocking information that contradicts the original decision.

The influence of our filters and our past experience results in another thinking trap. This is the "it's never happened before" trap. In many cases businesses have been caught in this trap, and blindsided by competitors who developed a product or process that was brand new.

In many situations this trap is more accurately described as the "it's never happened to me before" trap. An excellent book on the current American political and economic situation by Kevin Phillips called *American Theocracy* enumerates examples of economic declines in world powers. Phillips points out the common trajectories that these nations followed and the parallels to America in 2007. It was George Santayana who said: "Those who can not remember the past are condemned to repeat it." But of course you have to take an interest in learning history in the first place.

The "it's never happened before" trap is evident in much of the discussion around the decline in the world energy supplies. We certainly have never had a time in history when the world's primary source of energy was in decline and there was nothing to replace it. But just because something has never happened before does not mean that it cannot happen. The obvious example is products that are invented every day, from airplanes to computers, skyscrapers to iPods. The fact that something has never happened before can make it very difficult for people to get their heads around the idea, but it certainly does not prevent the event from happening.

The "calamitous consequences" trap is sometimes the driver behind using "it's never happened before" as a justification for a position. Using energy decline as an example, sometimes when I explain the possible longer-term consequences of energy decline my listeners respond with "but that would result in massive changes in our society." That is typically the point where they will invoke "and it's never happened before." The calamitous consequences trap adds unpleasantness to the never-happened-before scenario and thus makes it even less likely for our brains to embrace. On the other hand, if I told you about something that has never happened before but would have tremendous benefits, for example, teleportation technology as seen on *Star Trek*, you might doubt me but I imagine you would not want to dismiss me before you checked it out.

Another area where our brains deviate from logical, rational processing is in our bias towards extreme thinking. In our world there are many situations that are not black or white, right or wrong. In many of the important issues of the day there are at least several ways of looking at and analyzing the issues. Yet our brains gravitate to an analysis that lays things out as yes or no, right or wrong, us versus them. The principal advantage from a biological point of view of a simplified yes or no analysis is that it requires less physiological energy to be supplied to our brains. (Your children are correct when they say that thinking is hard work; conscious thinking requires greater blood flow to your brain.) Once we have decided whether we are on one side or the other, and put a simple label on the issue, we don't have to think about it anymore. We can make up our mind and stay there. This also means we tend to filter out any new information about the situation. At first we may have to consciously ignore the information, based on our earlier decision. But as time goes on, we build up our filter such that new contradictory information is blocked automatically. We know where we stand, and we know we are right, information to the contrary be damned.

Now if the issue in question is 1 + 1 = 2, then it is pretty clear, based on agreed upon conventions, whether we are right or not.

New information is extremely unlikely to change our position on the answer. And it shouldn't, since anyone who has learned arithmetic agrees that $1 + 1 = 2$. But if the issue is something where new information is continually being uncovered, then taking a position of simply ignoring new information is likely to result in bad decisions. (Stephen Harper, as Canada's prime minister, gave us an example of this type of position with respect to climate change. "We have a position that has a significant amount of support and more importantly, it's the only right position," stated Mr. Harper. If his words were to be believed, he was not open to new information and would never change his mind.)

Certainly absolutes apply in mathematics and logic. As well, we encounter situations every day where we look at information, make an analysis, and judge which is the best course to take. We may even label our decision as the "right way" or "wrong way" to do something.

What concerns me is how frequently this process is being reversed. The judgment is made first, and the evidence and analysis comes later, if at all. Then the positioning starts between the two sides, and the opponents use ridicule rather than rhetoric to try to score points. The goal is to get the momentum moving towards your extreme.

But the critical choice for us to make is not which side we are on. The critical choice is whether we accept this division in the first place — into good versus evil, right versus wrong. Do we accept a one-dimensional view of the world?

As I said, thinking is work. And it can be hard mental work to make the effort to understand the subtleties of an issue. But in many of the critical issues facing you, your organization, and our world, considering the shades of gray is what makes the difference between the less-effective and more-effective solutions.

Have you ever watched a child when they first learned to play peekaboo? At that stage of their mental development, they believe that by covering their eyes they can make objects disappear. They take great delight in having people and objects appear and disappear at will. These days I observe many adults behaving like children playing peekaboo. They seem to believe that if they close their eyes and ignore a problem, it will go away. I call this the "Ostrich Approach" where people would prefer to stick their heads in the sand rather than facing up to reality.

In my research and activities regarding energy supplies, I frequently encounter the Ostrich Approach. Many people I have met in the energy industry are aware that there are serious challenges facing Western society with respect to future energy supplies, but they prefer to ignore the issue. Politicians and the media as well, both with respect to energy and other tough issues, frequently take the Ostrich Approach. Of course, in many cases the politicians are simply reflecting the wishes of their constituents to not deal with the thorny issues of the day or especially of the future.

I have to admit that calling this approach of avoiding difficult problems the "Ostrich Approach" is a little unfair — to ostriches, since ostriches don't actually stick their heads in the sand. But the approach does work for people, at least in the short term. The reason it works relates back to the time continuum of past, present, and future. Since we only act and experience our lives in the exact present moment, ignoring a future problem feels better in the present and has no immediate consequences. Moreover we can come up with many reasons to justify why we don't need to take any action or expend any mental effort on dealing with the situation right now. These include:

- I don't believe it

- It may not happen

- It is too big a problem

- I can't do anything about it

- I can't make a difference to the situation

- It will happen anyway

- I'm too busy

- Why should I sacrifice if no one else is?

- My friends aren't worried about it

- Our leaders/experts aren't worried about it — and they should know

and so on...

Some of these relate to some of the specific thinking traps I address in this and other chapters. And once someone has decided to take the Ostrich Approach and starts enumerating their reasons then their filters kick in. Their unconscious brain collaborates by passing information that supports their reasons and blocking information that contradicts their Ostrich Approach.

But sooner or later reality will intrude. Often the use of the Ostrich Approach has made the situation worse with time. Maybe what was a small problem has become a big one, or a situation that could have been dealt with easily if addressed when discovered now requires massive mitigation. In my observation many people are using the Ostrich Approach regarding energy decline. Prominent people have pointed this out, but many leaders still have their heads in the sand.

The numerous thinking traps described in this chapter — recency, familiarity, anchoring, status quo, "it's never happened before," "calamitous consequences," and absolutes — have all evolved for good reason, because in most cases they are helpful. Especially during ancient times as human brains were evolving, when the world was both more simple and more dangerous for most humans, thinking this way prioritized information in the most useful manner. But in a more complex world, when our individual and collective actions can have consequences well beyond our own lives, we have to be wary of these ancient ways of thinking.

Thinking Collaboratively

Chapter 7

Why Don't They Get It?

So far this book has been about thinking from an individual's point of view. But of course we don't live in isolation. In fact, dealing with some of the significant challenges we face in the future will require us to work effectively together. And of course the key aspect of working effectively together is communicating with other people. If we had no filters, then when you and I looked at a situation we would both see the same information, process it logically, and reach the same conclusions. But as we have seen, our experiences, our biases, our assumptions that make up our filters will block or distort the information before we start to process it logically. And since you and I have different filters we're going to come to different conclusions.

A look at the following figure illustrates why considering our filters is so important for effective communications. If we look at the flow of information in a conversation between two people we see that the person on top in the diagram takes in the information through their filter, processes it, reaches their conclusions, and communicates the result to the other person. This communication then goes through the other person's filter, is processed, and communicated back, where it has to go through the first person's filter to complete the cycle. It is easy to see that if the two filters are very different there could be many words spoken but little information exchanged. And even the information that does get through someone's filter will be distorted by the filter and may be interpreted quite differently than how it was intended.

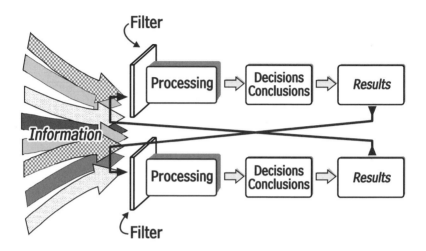

Sometimes the people involved in the discussion recognize that little information is flowing, and may try to increase the flow. Unfortunately problems often arise because the techniques used can end up being ineffective. For example, raising one's voice to increase the volume of the information may push some of it through the other person's filter. On the other hand, raising one's voice may result in the other person's filter shutting down even more. Repeating what you have said may help communications, if the problem was simply that the other person didn't hear. Conversely, repeating what you said may result in the person getting annoyed, once again shutting down their filter.

Looking at the model, there are two key conclusions that can be drawn. The first conclusion is that if the information you are trying to communicate is blocked by the other person's filter, they won't consider it. It doesn't matter how strong a case you have, how compelling or logical you believe your argument to be; if your information is blocked by their filter it will not be processed. That leads to the second key conclusion, which is that effective communications requires an understanding not just of your own filter (so that you can receive all of the information being sent to you) but of their filter as well. Since our filters govern most of our thinking process, it is apparent from the model that carrying on a conversation without examining the filters involved is likely a waste of time. If you are talking with someone whom you know well, for example a co-worker whom you see every day, you will have a pretty good idea of the characteristics of their filter and you may do this almost automatically. On the other hand, I have seen people who worked together for years who still didn't really understand each other because they had never examined the other person's filter. And of course, everyone has good days and bad days. You may know how they behave most of the time, but anticipating what might happen in any communication involves being aware of your assumptions. Sometimes, for a variety of reasons, the other person may not be open to the communication.

In a later chapter I will write in more detail about how to influence other people, but for now consider the industry that revolves around getting information through people's filters even when they don't want to listen. That industry of course is advertising. Advertisers specialize in getting their information through people's filters. They begin by studying the filters and then use techniques calculated to get their information through the filters.

Let's look at some of the techniques they use. Music is common in advertisements. It can work for a couple of reasons. One is that if the music is appealing or catchy people listen. The music, and with it the advertiser's message, passes through the filter. Another reason music works is if people like the artist who is performing the music then they are more likely to listen. The same thing applies for celebrity spokespersons — people listen to those they admire or respect. Humor is another technique — our filters tend to be more open if we are laughing or chuckling. Then there is the classic: sex. Finally, another technique is to be shocking, to present something that we don't expect, since an important function of our filter is to block out mundane information. If we consciously choose to ignore something several times, our filters will pick up on it and will automatically block out the same message when it occurs in the future. However, shocking messages tend not to be blocked. (There is a lesson here for companies trying to collect overdue bills. If you keep sending the same statement month after month it loses its effect. Try communicating in a different format or medium if you want to attract someone's attention.)

The media and others trying to influence us don't always use finesse. Sometimes they use the brute force approach to get information through our filters, what I call the Parrot Principle. The Parrot Principle repeats the same message over and over to accomplish two goals: get the message through the filter and then make the message stick. By constantly repeating the same message, the message provider wears down the filter's ability to block the message. Once a message does get through the filter it makes an impression. The more times something is repeated, the greater the count registered by the brain and the more likely the brain will accept it as true. Even if there is significant evidence contradicting the information, the fact that it is repeated over and over again tends to result in its acceptance. That is one of the real dangers of not being aware of the Parrot Principle. Often it is used when the message has little resemblance to reality (and that is why it is needed.) Sometimes it is used to propagate outright lies. These days some people seem to believe that lies told often enough and loudly enough will become the truth. Or maybe they are just succumbing to their own use of the Parrot Principle.

The Parrot Principle works best when there is a void to be filled. If people have already heard a counter viewpoint, their filters are already set to some extent. It is much harder to change a set filter than create a new one. It also helps if there is some appeal to the position being put forward in that it either presents something good or avoids something bad. The influence of our filters results in us being very susceptible to something we want to hear, even if logically we don't believe it. The familiar quotation, "There's a sucker born every minute," is both a description of the Parrot Principle and an example of it, since most people believe (as I did before I researched it) that it was said by P.T. Barnum. In fact its origin is somewhat uncertain, but years ago the Parrot Principle took over and now just about everyone believes it was said by Barnum. Lottery tickets are an interesting combination of the way our brains process statistics and the Parrot Principle. The Parrot Principle is invoked by providing frequent images of people winning lots of money. Some of the charity lotteries in our city emphasize the number of large prizes to be given away. This triggers the frequency processing of our brain — there are a lot of prizes, so there must be a good chance of winning! Then, for those who do think of the statistical view (that is they mentally divide the number of prizes into the number of tickets), organizers include a line such as the odds of winning are one in three. But of course the odds of winning the prizes they are featuring are not one in three.

Often the Parrot Principle is used to change a message significantly. The government of George W. Bush did this in its justification for the war in Iraq. In the early days, the war was about weapons of mass destruction. After that reason was discredited it became about bringing freedom and democracy to the Iraqi people. And although commentators and critics pointed out the inconsistency, because our memories fade, in fact the Parrot

Principle can be used effectively in these situations. One defense in our modern multimedia world is the recordings of what people actually said. The television program *The Daily Show with Jon Stuart* has, over the years, produced a large volume of comedy based on pointing out how these reasons have changed by playing video clips of past pronouncements.

The Parrot Principle can backfire if the user doesn't think ahead and anticipate the consequences if the message is believed. Politicians have discredited their own profession by continually raising issues of scandal or corruption. Although statistically a very small percentage of politicians are corrupt, many short-thinking politicians try to make political hay by hammering away when there is any hint of scandal. Voters may then see several days of media coverage on a small incident, but because of the frequency of reports the impression of many scandals is reinforced. Since pretty well all parties have some members who behave in arguably questionable ways, all politicians get painted with the same brush.

Finally, a few words on the word filter itself. The word filter is a very neutral word. People have told me that using the model, in particular the word filter, helped create an awareness about the differences in opinions and beliefs without triggering the defensiveness that sometimes arises regarding the words opinion and beliefs. For example, if a group of people are brainstorming new ideas and Bob's response to Jim's idea is "that's your opinion, here's what I think" Jim's reaction might be to take offence and/or defend his idea. But if Jim and Bob are both aware that they have filters, that the filters are essential as well as different, Bob could say "that's your filter, here's my filter on the situation." Both of them are more likely to recognize and appreciate the different conclusions they draw from the same information. Using the word filter reminds them of the model of thinking and the path of information in the conversation and facilitates a dialogue about the differences.

Even after you have decided to make that extra effort to understand and communicate with someone else there is an additional challenge. Not only do we have different filters with respect to the type of information we receive, we all have different filters as to the meaning of the words that are used to communicate this information. If you asked a number of people about the meaning of words like *purple* or *red*, as I often do, you would probably get pretty good agreement. But what about the meanings of words like *sometimes* or *often*? If you interact with children (and some adults!) you'll recognize that even yes or no can have flexible meanings to them. In normal conversations, words that have very precise dictionary definitions such as *always* and *never* end up being used in situations where they don't mean 100 percent of the time or 0 percent of the time. In many of my presentations I ask my audience members what they think different words such as *rarely*, *often*, *always*, and *never* mean. I'm still often surprised at the results — as a scientist, my definition of the word *always* is 100 percent of the time, while many of my audience members believe it means 85, 90, or 95 percent of the time. The point is not to get hung up on whether their definition or my definition is correct (besides, I know mine is!); the point is that we are using different definitions. They may have found that in the context in which they encountered the word *always*, a practical definition for them (and the intended meaning when they frequently hear the word) is 95 percent of the time. As an example, consider the classic phrase "the customer is *always* right." While it sounds pithy and has more impact than "the customer is almost always right," or "the customer is always right, up to a point," I suspect there are few people who would argue that the customer is right 100 percent of the time.

The colloquial use of absolute words in situations where their meaning isn't intended to be absolute can come back to haunt you as well. One Premier of Ontario found this out when he was first elected. He had promised not to raise taxes, a pretty clear absolute. Either you do raise taxes or you don't raise taxes. But after he was elected, he found out that the province's finances were not as sound as he expected. (Whether or not he did proper due diligence in investigating the province's finances before he made his promise is beside the point.) If he had more carefully anticipated the future — there's that one again — he would have realized that he needed to put a condition on his promise, or he might not have made the promise in the first place. Ironically, in the next election he was reelected principally for two reasons: one because most voters did realize that when he said "never" he really meant "never as far as he could see." The other reason was because his principal opponent also didn't look ahead and made what turned out to be an ill-considered promise regarding the funding of private religious schools.

In my presentations, when I ask people to define what they mean by *always*, *sometimes*, and *never* it is to illustrate two points. One is the differences that we all hold in our filters when it comes to the meaning of very common words. The second is to help people understand how imprecise language can be and raise their awareness of the language they use.

In my first book, *Thinking for Results — Success Strategies*, I describe the ACORN test, which can help raise your awareness of how casually you may use words such as *always* and *never*. (You can download an article on the ACORN test from our web site www.ThinkingforResults.com.) In this discussion I have focused on words that describe frequency of occurrence — such as *always*, *never*, *sometimes*. In many cases these words apply to fairly basic communications. But think of words that have emotion attached to them. As we saw earlier, words that trigger our emotional hot buttons can result in our reacting more quickly and less rationally. Working to understand someone else's filter, to truly see where they are coming from, is seldom easy. But by doing this you will increase the flow of information in your conversation and achieve your objectives more quickly. Ask yourself right now "who do I interact with where it would benefit me to better understand their filter?"

CHAPTER 8

INFLUENCING OTHERS' THINKING

After all of my study of how people make decisions, my observations of why people are motivated to do something, and my understanding of the thinking that leads people to conclusions, I have come to one inescapable conclusion: it all boils down to WIIFM. If you have ever attended any presentations on sales, or read any books on marketing you have likely run into the phrase WIIFM — *what's in it for me*. The bottom line is that human beings have necessarily evolved to act in their own self interest. The fact that we act this way is not right or wrong, it just is. So while people seem to be motivated by many different factors and act in support of different causes and philosophies, in the end they do what they do because of self-interest. There is a significant amount of research that bears this out, but working through a couple of examples will illustrate the point.

Even in altruistic actions, if you dig deeply into the motivation of the person performing the action, you will see there is a benefit for them. If a child is in trouble, most parents would put their life on the line for their child's safety. Part of that can be attributed to the hardwired response of humans to see their genes continue. But even with strangers, most of us would at least endure some inconvenience to help a stranger, for example, by providing a stranger with directions. In Western societies, voters pay taxes to fund public education for children they don't know. Most Western societies also pay taxes to fund public health care. And of course the ultimate example is a person who risks their life for a stranger. Ask these people why they took any of these actions and you'll likely hear answers like "it was the right thing to do." Probe a little deeper and they are likely to say "I feel good about helping someone else," or "I would feel bad if children couldn't get an education," or "if I hadn't helped out, I wouldn't be able to live with myself."

You will recognize that all of these responses depend on the individual's filter. Some people won't assist strangers, some don't believe in publicly funded health care. But there are few people who wouldn't help out a neighbor in a time of trouble and who wouldn't also have some expectation that their neighbor would help them out. Our upbringing affects our filters and the actions we take reflect the morals and values embedded in our filters. Some of this also depends on the idea of reciprocity. And a large portion of that depends on an individual's ability to anticipate the future. A person might say, "I don't have any kids — why should I pay for someone else's children's education"? or "I'm a healthy person — why should I pay more taxes to take care of someone else who is not very healthy?" Yet if they take the longer-term view and anticipate the future, they see it is in their self-interest to have educated young people and a health care system that will take care of them if they fall ill.

Thinking for Results and anticipating the future are based on practical observations of how people think, make decisions, and are motivated. So whether you agree with someone else's values and choices or not, if you are trying to influence them you need to begin by understanding their filter to find their motivators. Reviewing the communications model discussed in the last chapter is a good place to start when trying to understand what someone else may be seeking. The best way to find out what motivates someone else is to ask them. And then listen. If you really work with the concepts from the last chapter and this chapter, it is quite straightforward to determine what someone desires. As an example, for many years in several different areas I have used a "needs analysis" type of checklist during my initial contact with potential clients. (This is a technique I first learned from my colleague and friend Tom Stoyan, "Canada's Sales Coach." You can see an example of this at www.ThinkingforResults.com — the Thinking and Decision Making Checklist.) Underneath the question "What improvement do you need for greater results?" is a list of statements such as:

- consistently better decision making

- avoidance of mistakes by anticipating the future

- people who think more strategically

- improved group decision-making processes

- higher personal responsibility for outcomes

- better use of experience that exists in the organization

- people who see the big picture, not just the details

- improved problem-solving skills

- greater initiative in attacking problems

and so on...

This approach has three benefits. The first benefit (obviously) is that they tell me what they are looking for. After reviewing the list, I can provide them with an outline for a program customized to their particular need. You might be surprised — as I have been — at the number of times someone will come back to me and say "that's exactly what we want!" Of course it is exactly what they want, because they told me what they wanted; yet their response suggests this is not commonly done. The second benefit is related to the first but it is a little more subtle. You may have noticed that the statements are fairly vague. This is deliberate because the biggest benefit of the checklist comes when I discuss with the potential client each statement they have checked and ask them to explain what they had in mind when they checked it. When they checked an item on the list, they were looking at that statement through their filter. When I look at the statement, I am looking at it through my filter. For example, if we look at the third statement "people who think more strategically," I would bet that if you asked five people to explain what that statement means you would get five different answers. In asking for this clarification and in discussing the statements with the potential client, I not only clarify what they are looking for from the program but I also gain insights into their filter. (The approach of asking questions and listening to the answers to understand how someone thinks can be taken to a much more precise level of detail. A friend and colleague of mine, Shelle Rose Charvet, has written a book called *Words That Change Minds*, which is about understanding what motivates people by listening to their language. I highly recommend her book and her approach.) The third benefit of this approach is that it provides a framework to keep you on track. We are obviously more comfortable with our own filters, perspectives, and opinions than with someone else's filters. It can be very easy during a conversation for the other person to say a word or phrase that resonates with our filter and triggers our thinking in a certain direction. The checklist approach can help you keep from wandering off in your own favorite direction.

Once you have a good idea of someone else's filter, what should you do to influence them? Consider who influences you. Typically the people you listen to are the ones who have filters most similar to you. If you are attempting to influence someone who has a very different filter, one of the best ways to start is to make a connection by finding some common ground in your filters. Maybe it is a hobby or a sport that you both enjoy. Maybe it is a philosophy or the place you grew up. Even when you don't seem to have anything in common, there is a technique you can often use to find common ground. I will give you an example. Let's say we're chatting about what we do in our free time. I say I like to play soccer. You say you spend your time doing aerobics. The conversation might go like this:

ME: Aerobics? I find that really boring.

YOU: But with soccer, you have to commit to a schedule. You have to travel to the soccer field. With aerobics, I am free to do a workout whenever I feel like it.

ME: Yes, but for me the team aspect of soccer is what I enjoy, it keeps me motivated. I know that I've made a commitment to my team every week. That way, I get my exercise.

YOU: The flexibility of aerobics is what allows me to get in my exercise. Whenever I have 15 or 20 minutes, I can do a quick workout. That way, I get my exercise, and exercise is important.

ME: Yes, exercise is important.

You can see that even though we started with two different perspectives on what to do in our free time, in fact we both had the same goal. Having the conversation allowed us to identify the common ground. If this had been a real conversation I'm sure you can appreciate how we would now have a closer connection than we had when we started the conversation. As a result of that connection I am more likely to listen to you and you are more likely to listen to and be influenced by me. So a practical way to achieve the type of connection that leads to you being able to influence someone else is to explore what you have in common by taking the conversation to a higher level. This is shown in the diagram.

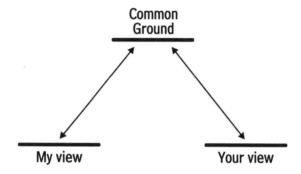

An exercise I often do in presentations is to have audience members pair up, each think of a noun, and then find a way, through conversation, to connect the two nouns. Invariably there is a way to create a connection (though some end up being quite bizarre!) This is the type of thing you can do to create that connection, the common link between you and the person you are attempting to influence. By using this technique, you can actually find common elements between positions that are diametrically opposed. Even such different philosophies as democracy and communism have some similar stated objectives, for example creating the best life for their citizens. Both in influencing people and in anticipating the future, the ability to find common connections is one of the keys to success.

CHAPTER 9

GROUPTHINK: COLLECTIVE FILTERING

Organizations, whether they are corporations, nonprofits, associations, governments, or even societies as a whole, are, in the end, simply collections of people. So when it comes to increasing the effectiveness of organizational thinking we need to look at thinking in three ways — thinking as individuals, thinking as individuals within the environment of a specific organization, and the way an organization itself "thinks."

An organization represents an environment in which each individual acts. Each person will bring their individual filters and thinking approaches to bear on the information they encounter in the organization. If they interact infrequently with the organization they will have minimal effect on the organization and vice versa. This is especially true if they are only occasionally involved with the organization, such as a store where they shop. If they are by nature polite, they will be polite when dealing with the sales staff. If they are by nature a jerk, they will likely be a jerk when they are interacting with a salesperson. In either case they will not have a large impact on the organization. Contrast that with individuals who are more regularly involved in a group. They will contribute to and form a part of the collective filter of the organization, group, or society. In a corporation we often call this filter the corporate culture. In a society, this collective filter includes beliefs, biases, morals, and societal norms, among other things. These collective filters are influenced by each individual and in turn influence the filters of the individuals, both inside the environment and to a lesser extent when the individual is removed from the group. As an example of the latter, someone who works in an organization with a very negative environment will likely come home in a bad mood and tend to see the world in a negative light.

These collective filters are very powerful because they govern the organization's or society's collective view of the world. They can differ significantly even between very similar organizations.

As an example, consider what happens when a new employee starts at a company. (Think about your own experience in this situation when you first started a job.) You knew little about the company and the norms of conduct. You may not even have known where the washroom was located. Your filter regarding the company was very open. As a result, you had to consciously process all the information you encountered, and you experienced information overload because you hadn't developed a filter to automatically select and prioritize information. Many companies have an orientation program to help new employees with this information overload. They may provide manuals, newsletters, and other information to educate the new employee about the organization. But an additional orientation occurs when the new employee mingles at the water cooler or is introduced around the office. Let's listen in on one of these orientations as Jim the veteran introduces Pat the new employee to some of the people at the organization. Jim and Pat start with the accounting manager.

JIM: Pat, I'd like you to meet Richard, our accounting manager. Richard runs a tight ship. Richard, this is Pat.

RICHARD: Nice to meet you, Pat.

PAT: Nice to meet you as well. [Pat and Jim leave Richard, and Jim chats as they walk away down the hall.]

JIM: Talk about a tight ship, he is so tight you have to get a signature for a paper clip. [Next, Jim and Pat encounter Bobby.]

JIM: Pat, this is Bobby, our sales manager. Bobby is a really friendly guy.

BOBBY: Hey there Pat, how are you doing on this fine day!

PAT: Fine, thank you, Bobby. [Once again as Pat and Jim walk away, Jim adds some commentary.]

JIM: Talk about friendly — you should've seen how friendly Bobby was at the Christmas party!

Many orientations have a similar flavor to this fictional one. There really are two components to the orientation — the official one, and the unofficial one. The official one covers where equipment is located, where people sit, and people's titles. But the unofficial one is where a new employee starts to get a real feel for the organization's filter. Give a new employee a few weeks, and they will have figured out that Bill is the smart one, Joe is the troublemaker, and whatever you do, don't cross Mary on a Monday morning. In some organizations if you don't arrive before 8:00 a.m. and leave after 7:00 p.m. you are a slacker. In other organizations people putting in anything more than a 9-to-5 day are considered to be playing up to management. I'm sure you can think of many examples of collective filters in your workplace and other organizations you belong to, let alone in your society.

Furthermore, just like the filters of the people who make up the organization, organizational filters are not necessarily rational or consistent. But the information that flows into the organization will be passed, blocked, or modified by the organizational filter, or more precisely by each person's interpretation of the organizational filter. Certainly an organization's mission, vision, and values can be useful in shaping this organizational filter, with the caveat that because many vision, mission and value statements are fairly general, they are also open to much individual interpretation. Having a value of "doing business in an ethical manner" will almost certainly result in different interpretations of *ethical* from different people. Other such descriptors would be "treat our suppliers fairly," "delight our customers," "innovative," "outstanding," and "client focused." It is apparent that each of these phrases is open to individual interpretation. Thus if the purpose of your vision and mission statements is to create a well-defined, clear organizational filter then you should use precise language with clear meanings in your statements.

Similar dynamics occur in project teams. If the team is composed of people who have worked with each other extensively, getting a new team on the same page may be fairly straightforward — people may not like each other, but they do know each other. On the opposite end of the spectrum are the increasingly common virtual teams, comprised of people from around the world who may never meet face-to-face. A colleague of mine, Claire Sookman, specializes in helping virtual teams work well together. A large part of that work involves clarifying team goals and guidelines for conduct. In essence the process involves consciously and deliberately creating a team collective filter, making explicit the expectations that would otherwise develop in an ad hoc manner.

When someone is involved with an organization frequently or to a greater extent, their "general-purpose filter" will be modified by their "organization-specific filter." If Harry usually acts like a jerk, it is likely he will be a jerk at work, but he might be a jerk in a different way. In fact, because Harry knows the people at work better than most people he may be a more annoying jerk. Your co-workers likely know many of your strengths as well as your weaknesses. In some cases co-workers may be better at pushing your buttons (and might be more motivated to do so) than your friends or family.

The fact that the organizational filter is created by and perpetuated by a group of people is why organizational change can be so difficult. Even if a few people are convinced there is a better way to view a situation and would like to change the filter, they are likely to encounter substantial resistance from the majority who have an investment in the current system (even if the investment is simply familiarity.) It is hard enough to change one person's filter; it is much harder to change a collective filter. And of course because everyone at the organization sees the world through that same filter, new ideas tend to get blocked before they are considered. Moreover, those who have been around a long time and who have the least-malleable filters are often the ones who remember failed initiatives from the past. "Oh yeah, we tried that before and it didn't work," can be a common refrain.

One of the keys to organizational change is to remember that it's not simply a case of changing the plaque on the wall with the new mission, vision, and values. It is usually tougher to change the unofficial filter than the official directives. Just because the filter is not written down doesn't mean it can be ignored, though this is frequently what happens. When I work with an organization my work often involves helping people in the organization identify these collective filters. It often takes an outside viewpoint to see the filters that the members of the organization cannot see. Collective filters are a big reason why organizations keep seeing and doing things the same way over and over again, even when some people realize there is a better way to do things. New information or approaches get blocked by the organization's filter. Feedback as well is stopped before it reaches the organization's analysis.

This can be especially true regarding assumptions made about the marketplace, sales, and customers. In an established business it is easy to fall into a trap of extrapolation and to project the past into the future. Even if new intelligence is presented — say, for example, the emergence of a new competitor — it is common for the filter to block out the importance of the information if not the information itself. The organizational filter often becomes a reinforcing feedback loop. When people are hired, they tend to be hired because they have a filter similar to the organization's existing filter. Then when an idea is generated, not only does it come from someone looking through the organization's filter, but it is also evaluated by people who started with similar filters. This is probably the most compelling reason for encouraging your people to attend conferences and external seminars. Involvement in professional associations is also a great way to see your world through the eyes of someone from a different workplace. Sometimes the impact of these insights is limited because only a small number of people from your organization attend the conference. They return with great ideas but run into the organization's old filter. My suggestion to managers who want to get the most value from people attending conferences is that you ask them to report on the conference when they return. Conferences can be a great place to find out about unrecognized trends that may affect your organization in the future.

I like to encourage people to go even further than that. Get involved in groups that have a true diversity of members and opinions. This might happen through common interests in another field such as a hobby or a sport. (I meet a wide range of people from different backgrounds through my sailing.) Hang out with people who have broad interests and knowledge. If you are middle aged, talk to young people. If you are young, don't just hang out with young people. These are all ways of seeing the world through someone else's filter. In the process you will gain a greater understanding of both the world and your own filter.

In societies there many examples of collective filters, some of which are not very helpful. Collective filters can lead to collective blindness. We believe that our position and approach are correct and our opposition's are incorrect, though an impartial third person might have a difficult time distinguishing between the rationale we both use. When we do something, it is okay; when someone else does the same, it is not okay. Nowhere is this more apparent than in international conflict. When our foreign army arrives in a sovereign country, there is a good reason for it; when someone else's army lands in a sovereign country, it is an invasion. In fact, I don't think there is any area of human relations where we see more contradictions between words and actions than in international relations. But because we as citizens of each country look at the world through our national filters, we justify our actions and claim we are the ones thinking correctly.

In society the creation and manipulation of the collective filter is often carried out covertly as well as overtly. National celebrations, teaching history in school, cultural events, politicians, and the media are all involved in shaping a society's collective viewpoint. Unfortunately, in my opinion some of these influences are not as useful as they used to be. Political debate in many Western countries has degenerated from discussion of issues and reasoned arguments to personal attacks. With some exceptions the mainstream media spends less time on in-depth coverage and more time skimming the surface and competing for unique stories, especially stories with "winners" and "losers."

In the Western world today, advertising and public relations have a huge influence in shaping societal filters. One of the largest shifts in the United States and Canada in the last two decades has been to the so-called market economy. Some of this shift has been attained through the use of the Parrot Principle. A frequent message from corporations and from many governments, communicated through the media, has been that private industry is more efficient than government and that markets should be allowed to run with minimal regulation. This significant shift is discussed in more detail in the last chapter on world events.

And no discussion of modern societal influencers would be complete without mention of the Internet. In some respects the Internet is the antithesis to the collective filter — it is a place where individuals, at least in most countries, can get their own message out without it being filtered by the media. There certainly are some wackos on the Internet (there is my filter showing through!) But there are also some very reasoned discussions that don't occur anywhere else. There are issues, several of which I will talk about in the last chapter, which most people never consider because our leaders and the media don't seem to want to talk about them. I don't want to sound like a conspiracy theorist; I think in at least some cases the media ignores issues because they believe they are too complicated and not of enough interest to the average person. On the other hand, there are issues such as energy decline which will affect all of us and where the Internet is the only place these issues are being addressed in any depth.

The other area in which I would like to see more media attention is that of increasing everyone's understanding of other societies. I guess the hopeful aspect of this situation is that there is the potential for people around the world to go deeper and find the aspects of our collective filters on which we can agree. Occasionally there are science fiction movies describing an invasion by a society from outer space. In most cases the countries of the world band together to defeat the common foe. In these plots the collective filter is common to everyone around the world, and is similar to the approach of finding common ground when influencing others. Of course, we don't have to go to outer space to see examples of coalitions formed during wartime between countries that have little in common during peacetime.

As someone who believes that inward-looking collective filters limit thinking and can lead to problems, let me make a couple of suggestions as to how to expand these filters. On an international level, probably the most helpful way to change a filter is travel. My appreciation of other aspects of the world, other societies, and the commonality we share has been enhanced by the travel I have done. As we face an increasingly resource-strained world, travel may become more difficult, in which case I would suggest the next best thing is to socialize with people who originally came from different cultures. I am fortunate to live in Toronto, a city where many residents have come from other parts of the world. This allows me to learn about their cultures and their views on the world. Does it matter? After all, it is a lot easier to get along with people who have the same filters as you. True, but I believe that whether you are looking at organizations or societies there can be huge benefits in obtaining input from people with a wide range of filters, rather than simply bringing together like-minded people. The complex problems we face in our organizations and in our societies are better dealt with by welcoming a wide range of perspectives. If the only people asking and answering the questions all have the same background, experience, and viewpoint, you end up with the kind of myopia that resulted in the stock market crash in 2001.

Besides, sometimes you just need a wide variety of knowledge. Stop for a moment to look at the next figure and see if you can interpret the meanings of these five different items. These five items each represent a fairly specialized piece of information from a range of disciplines and experiences. Since I created the list, I know the meaning of all five. But it is quite unlikely that another individual would have exactly the same interests and experiences as me. When I use this in a presentation it is extremely rare to find anyone who knows what all five mean. On the other hand, a group of more than about 30 people usually can combine their knowledge to identify the meaning of all five.

1.

2. **Em7**

3. **The Seven Summits**

4. **Burrard Inlet**

5. **Rikki Don't Lose that Number**

(I imagine some of you are curious, so let me explain the items. The first one is the word "Stormy" spelled out in the flags that ships and boats use for communication. I chose the word stormy in particular because the letters s-t-o-r-m-y are commonly used as signaling flags in sailboat races, so anyone who has ever raced sailboats would likely know these letters. Number two is a type of musical chord — an "E minor 7th." Number three, the Seven Summits, refers to the seven highest mountains on each of the seven continents. I learned about this when my wife climbed Mount Kilimanjaro, the highest peak in Africa. Number four, Burrard Inlet, is the harbor in the city of Vancouver, Canada. And finally, if you are from a certain generation, you will undoubtedly know that "Rikki Don't Lose that Number" is a song by the musical group Steely Dan.) These days with the Internet you could likely find the meaning of these five items without too much difficulty. But knowing what something means and understanding its significance are two different things. In business and in society there is often no substitute for firsthand knowledge and experience. Diversity in experience, approach, and style can certainly make working together more of a challenge. But I maintain it is a challenge worth accepting.

We don't always have to agree with each other, we don't always have to obtain consensus, and it is not always a zero-sum game where one person "wins" the argument and the other person "loses." Keep in mind the model from the last chapter and the idea of dialogue in addition to discussion. Examine not just the information flowing but the path and the filters through which it flows. Collective filters can strengthen an organization or be its limitation. And how we deal with collective filters worldwide will determine the future of our planet.

Chapter 10

Dramatically Improving Group Thinking

One of the ways I sometimes begin my presentations is with a humorous segment that asks the questions "Do you ever get frustrated with the bad thinking that goes on these days?" and "Why don't other people think as well as you do?" Although the questions are somewhat tongue-in-cheek, at some level most people agree that sometimes people in organizations don't think very well. I think there are three principal reasons why people in organizations don't think better:

- they are not encouraged to think
- they are not allowed to think
- they don't know how to think better

Number three on this list can often be addressed through books like this one and my previous book, and through seminars or workshops. Helping someone improve their thinking skills is often the easy part, since it only requires one person changing. The first two issues, on the other hand, are generally organizational issues. An example could be "don't think, just do your job." Of course, most of the time it is much more subtle than that, such as telling someone you want their input, but then ignoring it. Not giving them time or opportunity to present their point of view. Telling people to do something a new way while ignoring their reasons as to why the old way worked in the past. Or the converse — ignoring new ways of doing things and insisting it be done the way it always has been done.

As is the case for many systems, if maintenance is neglected the organizational filters and the quality of organizational thinking will deteriorate. Perhaps it has something to do with human nature, but it certainly seems that good news and positive developments tend to be forgotten more quickly than bad news. Thus it is worthwhile spending some time, money, and effort celebrating successes. Don't go over the top because that can lead to cynicism, but deliberately pointing out positive events reinforces the aspects of the organizational filter that resulted in those outcomes.

As usual, the Ostrich Approach in the event of setbacks rarely works in the long run. People will find out or figure out what is going on and if you ignore the reality the organizational filter becomes "management has no grasp of reality." In one project I was working with a manager who said her boss told her "I don't like it when you bring me a problem I can't solve." That strikes me as sort of a preemptive Ostrich Approach — you don't need to bury your head in the sand if the problem never gets near your sandbox.

I developed a roadmap to help people improve the thinking in their organizations. This is shown in the figure on the next page.

Although it is worthwhile to set a goal of improving everyone's thinking in all situations, in practice it is typically easier to tackle learning with a specific example. Thus the first step in this roadmap is to identify a specific area where you would like people to improve their thinking. Maybe you are looking for people who see more of the big picture, rather than focusing on the details. Or maybe you are looking for people who understand the importance of details that may have been missed in the past. Maybe you are looking for better group decision making and collaboration.

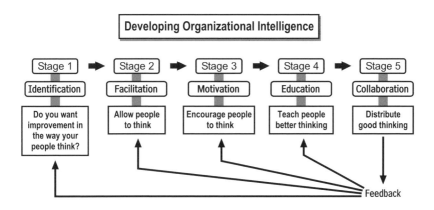

Maybe you would like to increase the flow of important information and/or reduce the flow of unimportant information. Maybe you are looking for new and unique solutions to old problems, getting unstuck from "we always do it this way." (For a comprehensive list, look at the Thinking and Decision Making Checklist at www.ThinkingforResults.com that I mentioned earlier.) Once you have identified an area in which to focus, the next step is to facilitate better thinking. This means identifying barriers to good thinking.

A classic example is the sales manager who would like more cooperation between members of his sales team but who awards bonuses based on individual performance. Another example would be asking people to be more innovative in their approaches but then requiring them to follow existing procedures. Part of the original intent of business process re-engineering as described by Michael Hammer and James A. Champy in their groundbreaking book *Re-engineering the Corporation: A Manifesto for Business Revolution*, was to redesign business processes such that people and equipment could operate more efficiently. (Business process re-engineering got a bad name when many organizations used it as a synonym for layoffs.) But the original goal was to rethink the way the process was assembled.

A book that I consider my favorite, and in my opinion possibly the best business book on strategy and improving organizational effectiveness is *The Fifth Discipline* by Peter Senge. It enjoyed tremendous popularity during the early 1990s, but fell from favor (I believe) because it required a significant amount of thinking to implement the ideas. In business, as in personal life, people are often looking for the simple, quick, pre-packaged solution. It is easy to fall into the trap of spending more time seeking a quick solution than it would take to think your own situation through. By all means, get input and help from experts, but make sure you spend the time to develop a solution for your particular situation. The intent of *The Fifth Discipline* was to analyze the structure of business systems and identify components of business systems such as feedback loops, side effects, limits to growth, escalations, and unintended consequences. By identifying the components you can anticipate the behavior of your system as well as the most effective places to intervene to achieve the outcomes you seek. In many cases small changes in the system can result in significant improvements in organizational thinking. There are examples in the book that illustrate how rational people making rational decisions may still end up with an outcome that in the final analysis is far from optimal.

Identifying barriers to improving thinking can be a challenge because once again you are looking at your organization through your organizational filter. But identifying and removing these barriers can result in significant improvement in organizational performance. Furthermore, working at improving the later stages in the map (encouraging people to think, or teaching them tools for better decisions) without removing barriers to thinking will make the situation worse, not better, by frustrating employees.

This is another good reason for tackling the improvement of organizational thinking in small chunks, because you can clearly focus on removing barriers in that specific area. Only once the major barriers to thinking are removed should you move on to the next stage of the map — motivating people — encouraging them to think.

There are several time-tested ways to do this, such as the use of employee suggestion programs. These suggestion programs can be a double-edged sword however; if you ask for suggestions but do nothing with the suggestions provided it can be worse than not asking in the first place. On the positive side, there are many examples of organizations who have had significant success through employee suggestion programs. Some programs provide monetary rewards based on the financial benefit to the organization. But studies have shown that money is not the principal motivator of most people. For many people, recognition is the most important thing. Combining financial rewards with recognition gives the best of both.

The best way to motivate people and encourage them to think better is to use the techniques outlined earlier on influencing people. Help them see how using their heads more will improve the situation for them. A commitment to act on their suggestions can go a long way to making this happen. Even a seemingly small thing, like giving people more choice as to how their work station is arranged, can lead to big payoffs, both in their assessment of the organization (improving their organizational filter) and in their individual productivity.

Addressing these first three stages in the roadmap demonstrates that you are committed to using your people's brains as well as their brawn. When you give people this opportunity, they often recognize for themselves that they could use techniques and training on how to think better. Helping them understand their thinking processes, providing analysis tools, and assisting them with information gathering are all ways to help them improve their thinking. Since basic thinking techniques can be taught in a one day seminar, organizations are often tempted to start at stage four. It is certainly easier to send people to a seminar than to do the work of the earlier stages. But as noted before, improving people's thinking before they have the opportunity to practice better thinking will cause frustration.

Stage five represents one of the principal reasons we create organizations in the first place — to collaborate. Collaboration in successful organizations is much more than putting together a set of skills. It is also about having people with the same skills but different filters review problems and opportunities. It is about bringing together that diversity of views and skills from different levels of the organization, not simply from the top down. Collaboration involves working together on the challenges and then sharing the knowledge that has been developed during this work. This collaboration does not have to be a complex process; sometimes a simple bulletin board can be an essential component of collaboration. You may have encountered the situation where you struggled with a problem for a significant amount of time only to find out that a colleague had encountered the same problem and found a solution just a week before — but you didn't know about it. These don't have to be huge problems — something as simple as figuring out how to get a document to print on a specific printer down the hall might be one of those problems where several people end up duplicating their efforts because there is no convenient way to share the solution. By posting a simple note on an electronic or physical bulletin board one person could save several co-workers hours of frustration.

Finally, at every stage of the process there is the opportunity for feedback. Feedback is one of the goals of the process of developing organizational thinking. As people work through this process they will identify barriers, motivators, and skill or knowledge gaps that can be addressed to continually improve the organization's thinking.

PREPARING FOR THE FUTURE

Chapter 11

How Can You Shape the Future?

I have long been fascinated by stories built around the idea of time travel. If someone could travel into the future and then back to the present, could they influence the future? Wouldn't that mean that they couldn't travel to the future they traveled to? What about traveling into the past to affect the present? From a practical point of view, time travel seems extremely unlikely. But how much can we influence the future? Even in the short term can we change the current direction of our societies? I certainly hope so. One of the principal reasons I'm writing this book is because I see organizations and societies headed in directions where they seem to have little concern for the future. My hope is that these directions can be changed by people working together, gathering all possible information, and doing serious analysis of where we're headed. And I hope that when the analysis is done that people won't dismiss it simply because it is unexpected or inconvenient.

There are certainly many forces that oppose change. Inertia born from familiarity is probably the top one, for several reasons. When we are used to doing something, when we have set up our habits and assumptions (our filters), doing something new is a lot more work. It is much easier to keep doing things the same old way. Often there are vested interests that have something to lose (such as financial investments, power, or reputations) in the event of a change.

Furthermore, once we have invested the time, money, and effort in doing something a certain way, it usually makes sense to keep doing it that way unless there is an overriding reason to do things differently. Our brains have evolved to match our current situation with past experiences, and will always favor the status quo. Still, major change in societal direction can be achieved. Typically it occurs through one of two ways. One is through concerted, long-term, rational discussion and action. An example of this is changes in attitude about drinking and driving. The other way is through a discontinuous change typically provoked by a shocking event. Author Naomi Klein wrote the book *The Shock Doctrine* describing this type of change and pointing out how vulnerable people can be when faced with shocking situations. Both these changes are achieved by changing people's filters. I will address each of these in turn.

When I was a young driver, perceptions around drinking and driving were just starting to shift. Prior to, and to some extent during, the 1970s it was not uncommon to hear someone boast "I got really drunk last night, I don't know how I managed to drive home." MADD (Mothers Against Drunk Driving) was formed in 1980 after the founder lost a child to a drunk driver and discovered that drunk driving was not being treated seriously, in fact it was not even in most people's awareness. Over the next two decades MADD expanded across the United States and into Canada. They have been steadfast in their goals of educating politicians and the public and working for changes in legislation to reduce alcohol-related injury and death. Through a combination of strong appeals to emotion by people who had lost loved ones or were severely injured by drunk drivers, and the presentation of solid statistics MADD, along with partners such as government agencies, has changed the societal filter regarding drinking and driving. As a result, the number of alcohol-related traffic deaths in the United States dropped from 30,000 in 1980 to about 17,000 in 2007.

MADD's approach worked for two reasons. One, it used emotions to open up people's filters to a rational argument — that it was criminal to allow a drunken person to get into a car and as a result kill or maim an innocent person. The second reason was because it was a concerted effort over a long period of time. Each year the public and legislators would move a little bit more in support of their cause. Fortunately they had the longevity and dedication to continue their campaign. If someone from 1970 were to travel in time to today, I expect they would be astounded by today's attitudes about drinking and driving. MADD succeeded by making small and consistent changes in people's filters each year.

Another example is the large number of regions that have banned smoking. In Toronto where I live you are no longer allowed to smoke in any restaurant, bar, or public building. A decade ago this would have been unheard of. But once again it started with separate smoking areas, led to separate smoking rooms, and worked up to the comprehensive ban.

A different process affects our filters during times of severe shock. At these times of great discontinuity, such as September 11, 2001, people's filters are so overwhelmed by unexpected information that they question large portions of their filters. Their present is so out of alignment with their past that they don't know what to believe. At these times, as Naomi Klein points out, people are susceptible to influences and actions that they might normally question or resist. You could think of it as the event metaphorically blowing a big hole in their filter. But since people can't survive without their filters they are looking for something new to replace their old beliefs, the ones shattered by the event. Klein warns that in the past governments and other organizations have taken advantage of people's vulnerable states to enact legislation that limits rights or to profit in ways that normally wouldn't be accepted. The book stresses that we need to be prepared because Klein expects shocks to increase in the future.

I agree with Klein that it is likely we will see more discontinuities in the near future than we have seen for a long time. There are many unstable geopolitical forces, there are environmental and energy issues, as well as economic situations where we are heading into uncharted waters. More than most times I believe it is important to understand how individuals and societies view the future, how current conditions and past experiences influence that view, and how you can be prepared by anticipating and influencing the direction that the future takes. I think this is more than just a case of maximizing our short-term effectiveness. I believe we have a responsibility to ourselves and future generations to become aware of the changes that are happening. History has shown that societies who become complacent and unaware of their assumptions end up vulnerable to decline. A thorough discussion of this issue is covered in the book *American Theocracy*, the book I mentioned earlier that I highly recommend.

Chapter 12

Avoiding Future Thinking Traps

When we look to the future — whether we are attempting to predict or anticipate — there are more thinking traps that affect our conclusions. Once again they come from a combination of the evolution of our brain and the database of our past experiences.

In addition to affecting our views of the present, the previously discussed "it's never happened before" and the "it's never happened to me before" traps often affect our view of the future, especially when combined with the "calamitous consequences" trap.

A common thinking technique in humans, which sometimes becomes a thinking trap, is extrapolation. From the moment we are old enough to perceive our surroundings, the majority of situations we observe are events where extrapolation can be applied. We push a ball, it starts rolling and keeps rolling in the same direction. We see a person disappear behind an object and reappear on the other side. We learn that small noises don't attract much attention, but that the louder we wail the faster someone is likely to attend to our needs. As we grow older we learn how to throw a ball, drive a car, and observe many other physical events that lend themselves to the idea of prediction using extrapolation. Eventually we do learn of some situations where extrapolation doesn't work. For example, a little wine makes you feel good, a little more makes you feel better, but a lot of wine ends up making you feel bad!

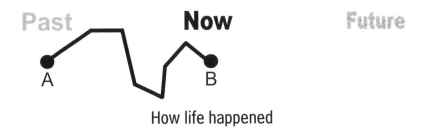

How life happened

Another characteristic of our thinking that affects and reenforces our use of extrapolation is the way we remember the past. Looking at the figures, an accurate historical record of how we reached the present from a point in the past might look like the first diagram. There are typically many twists and turns on the way from A to B. But partly because our memories fade, and partly because

Our memories fade

of the limited capacity of our brains, when we look back we tend to remember a straight line. We "back extrapolate" in a way that makes it seem obvious how we got here from there. Then when we think ahead, we extrapolate this remembered past into the future:

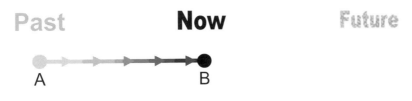

How we remember it happening

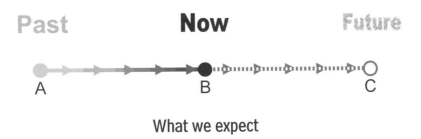

What we expect

Since human brains evolved in an era when most observable phenomena were physical phenomena, extrapolation is one of our hardwired thinking strategies. Marketers use this knowledge to great effect, a common example being the marketing of investments. At the end of every brochure or commercial, advertisers are required to state something like "Past performance does not guarantee future results." So if past performance is not a guarantee of future returns, why do they keep talking about past performance? It is largely to appeal to the extrapolation function of your brain. If you are presented with information that shows that for the past five years a certain investment has had phenomenal returns, the extrapolation mechanism in your brain automatically assumes that performance will continue. The conscious part of your brain processes the disclaimer, but the extrapolation part looks at the data and comes to its own conclusion. This can be especially effective if the information is presented as a graph, with a nice upward-trending line, rather than as a simple table of numbers.

There is also an extremely important distinction between the different types of extrapolation we might carry out. All extrapolation in the physical world tends to be either linear or limited. By linear I mean that the rolling ball does not increase in speed — if it travels one foot in one second we expect it to travel the next foot in one second. By limited I mean physical situations where the speed is not constant, for example an accelerating vehicle, but there is still a limit to the speed it will reach. In the physical world we don't expect that if we put our foot on the accelerator and hold it there for an hour that our automobile would eventually travel at the speed of sound. Yet when people are drawing graphs as lines on paper or pixels on the computer screen, it is common to see the graphs extend upward with no limit. An example of this is a presentation I encountered on the Internet, created by an energy professional from the United States Energy Information Agency (U.S. EIA) in 2005. His prediction was that there was no need to worry about oil supply for at least 50 years because unconventional sources of oil, such as the oil sands in Alberta, Canada, could be expanded. As proof he had done a mathematical analysis where he fitted past- and near-term predictions of production from the oil sands and projected them into the future. Using a six percent compounded growth rate his prediction was that by 2070 there would be more oil coming each day from the oil sands than was produced each day in 2005 *in the whole world*. This would be an expansion of oil sands production by over 80 times. Anyone who knows anything about the oil sands (and I would've expected someone from the U.S. EIA to know something about the oil sands) recognizes that while it is truly an awesome resource in volume, the oil is extremely difficult to extract and refine. Even at the levels of production back in

2005 there was severe strain on water supplies, and the production techniques required an enormous amount of natural gas. The idea that daily production could be expanded by 80 times simply because the mathematics said so was ludicrous.

On the other hand, our bias to linear or limited motion and growth — because that is what we experience every day — leaves us blind to one area where projection can be extremely useful. That area is compound or exponential growth. Author and physicist Albert Bartlett writes and lectures on sustainable living. He maintains "The greatest shortcoming of the human race is our inability to understand the exponential function." While the details can be debated, exponential growth (or contraction) is certainly extremely important when looking to the future. Population growth and demand for resources are two areas that can experience compound growth, and we have seen the results in the increase in world human population over the past two centuries.

There are two aspects to the exponential growth function that people tend to miss because we don't experience it every day — the first is that, as mentioned before, physical acceleration always reaches a limit. For example, exponential growth is used to predict an optimistic scenario for the future, without taking into account physical or other limits. The projection for oil sands production described above would be an example. Another example would be financial calculations that predict how much you will earn in interest 30 years from now. This type of situation tends to occur when we are looking for a positive outcome from the projection such as market size or growth of resources.

The second situation is when we don't recognize the power of the exponential function — no pun intended. Seven percent growth compounded over ten years results in a doubling from the initial number. Think of that in terms of the population of a city or town. Even five percent growth over a short six years is an increase of over one third. In a society obsessed with growth, especially economic growth, these are numbers to keep in mind.

The compounding works during decline as well. A five percent reduction over fourteen years results in less than half the original resource.

Extrapolation can be a useful tool when we understand how and where to use it. But too often, because it seems so intuitive, people fail to take into account both its power and its limitations.

These future thinking traps are traps precisely because they work in so many situations of our everyday experience. They are intuitive. If our lives still consisted of dropping rocks, throwing spears, and running and jumping, this type of thinking would be all we would need. But the complexity of the societies we live in now requires a closer examination and a more thorough analysis of the projections we are making. Relying on our intuition can and does lead us astray.

Throughout history there have been occurrences that humans have not been able to explain. In many instances these events were postulated to have been caused by supernatural beings or forces. It is part of human nature to try to discover or explain the reasons for something happening. My original field of study, physics, is all about explaining various aspects of the physical world. Humans like to understand why things happen in large part because it allows us to make predictions about the future.

Faith or belief is of course a part of someone's filter. If someone is religious, they will likely pray to their God or Gods in response to a difficult situation, for example when they encounter a physical or emotional hardship. If someone is not religious then there would be no point in them praying even when they encounter exactly the same situation — they have a different filter and as a result will reach a different conclusion, namely that prayer will have no effect.

My use of faith or belief in this context is not intended to be restricted simply to religious faith. In North America in recent decades we have seen a tremendous increase in belief in "free markets." There are numerous studies on both the strengths and weaknesses of free markets in various situations. Yet in the final analysis, both the strongest proponents and the strongest opponents to free markets are basing their positions largely on faith. There is no definitive way to "prove" whether minimizing market regulation is good or bad; there is evidence of both benefits and costs associated with a free market society. In my opinion a balance between the two extremes as practiced by some Western societies seems to provide the best lives for the most citizens.

In 2007 the movie and book *The Secret* were very popular. *The Secret* maintains that everything that happens to you in your life is a result of your thoughts; if you think positively and frequently about what you want to have occur, it will occur; if bad things are happening in your life it is because you are thinking negative thoughts.

While I agree that attitude, limiting beliefs, and focus do make a difference in your success, you cannot ignore the reality of your present situation. In fact there is an interesting asymmetry in the way the "law of attraction" is commonly presented — in order for good things to happen [in your future] you have to think good thoughts; if bad things have happened [in your past] it is because you were thinking bad thoughts. In this circular "logic," if you haven't got what you want yet, you just have to think about it more. Promoters of *The Secret* talk about how they were featured on Oprah twice in two weeks. They don't mention that the second show was scheduled because Oprah received a letter from a woman who was diagnosed with breast cancer. The woman wrote that "after much thought, I have decided to heal myself." Oprah (or possibly her lawyers) decided she needed to clarify her position on *The Secret*. If you visit Oprah's website you'll find she describes the law of attraction as a "tool" and not the answer to everything. And contrary to some proponents of *The Secret* she also emphatically states it is not "a get-rich-quick scheme." In what seems to me to be a realistic and practical approach Oprah says the law of attraction can help you decide what you want your life to be. Most importantly she says it can help you make "choices *through action* to create that life."

Whether someone's faith is in religion, free markets, or *The Secret*'s "law of attraction," the faith will act as a filter through which the believer views the information they encounter.

The common trap with faith is similar to invoking one's right to an opinion. It is often used when the person involved doesn't want to do the work or face the unpleasant conclusion of evidence-based analysis of the situation. Rather than address the problem of malnourished children, it is much easier to say "it is God's will," or "give them free markets, and they can work themselves out of poverty," or "they must have done something to attract that poverty." While the causes for poverty are many, and possible solutions even more numerous, the debate about what to do is not furthered by ignoring causes such as inequity in the random distribution of resources on our planet or lack of opportunity for education.

Probably the most disturbing use of faith or belief to me as a scientist is in "justifying" an assertion that completely contradicts both scientific and common knowledge. Here the approach is that something must be believed precisely because it cannot be proven. Traditional religion has relied on this approach through most of its history. Now new age movements such as *The Secret* are trying the same approach. However, having seen the problem that the advance of science has caused for traditional religion, New Age mysticism has attempted to co-opt science. Nowhere has this been more blatant then the confusion attempted regarding quantum physics.

Let's get a couple of things straight right up front. The development of quantum physics has not made traditional physics obsolete. Quantum physics is a modification to classical physics that deals specifically with objects and forces of very small dimensions, on the scale of molecules and atoms. Quantum physics does not replace classical physics, it simply refines classical physics in some special cases. But quantum physics does not apply to the type of objects we deal with every day. So just because two subatomic particles can occupy the same place at once, does not mean that you and I can physically occupy the same space at once.

Yet practically every day we see people who have no clue of physics, quantum or otherwise, stating that quantum physics makes possible all sorts of impossible events. While I was encouraged that a Google search of the terms "quantum physics" and "quantum mechanics" yield at least one page of legitimate physics references, the paid sponsored links on the right side of Google were as follows:

> quantum physics
> Understand the Secrets of Quantum Physics - Manifest the Life you want
> www....

> The Final Theory
> The best-selling book our scientists hope you never read. Find out why!
> www....

Quantum Changed My Life

"How Does The Secret Really Work?" The Answer Inside May Shock You!

www....

Quantum physics

Explode Your Potential With 7 Keys Of Quantum Physics & Mind Creation!

www....

Hear Dr. Quantum

The Secret and What the Bleep!? teacher on audio! Free sound clips.

www....

Quantum Mechanics

Seek The Truth Behind Real Life Mysteries. Paranormal State at A&E.

www....

Use Quantum Physics Now

Learn to Identify & Transform Your Subconscious Beliefs & Get Results!

www....

The Law of Attraction

It's still *The Secret* if you don't know how to use it.

www....

The approach in this instance is to claim that since quantum physics seems weird, but is true, then what ever else that is weird can also be claimed to be true. Setting aside the logical problem with this analysis (because one weird thing is true, I can claim anything else weird to be true as well), quantum physics only seems weird when viewed through our filters of common experience. Since our brains rely so much on analogies and relating our current situation to past experiences it is only natural to judge quantum physics as weird. But weird or not, it has proper experimental evidence supporting the theory. Quantum physics does not say that everyday science can be violated. And in important fields of study — such as building bridges, testing new drugs, or creating the voice recognition program I am using to dictate this book — praying, wishing, or discounting the scientific method will not achieve the outcomes we expect for our society.

Faith of one sort or another is a comfort for many people. Sometimes it motivates them to do universally accepted good deeds. But faith can also be a very narrow filter through which to view the world, and many bad deeds have been done in the name of faith.

As our world becomes more interconnected, disagreements between faiths become more common. The one factor that will affect all faiths is the intrusion of reality.

Chapter 13

Expanding Your Thinking: Wholeception

> The message is that there are known knowns; there
> are things we know that we know. There are known
> unknowns; that is to say there are things that we
> now know we don't know. But there are also
> unknown unknowns — there are things we do not
> know we don't know. And each year we discover a
> few more of those unknown unknowns.
>
> *Donald Rumsfeld*

I am not a fan of Donald Rumsfeld, but I think that this is one of
the smartest and most self-aware statements I have heard from
anyone in politics in a long time. The disappointing part is that I
don't think that the government of which Donald Rumsfeld was a
part recognized the importance of this statement.

The government of George W. Bush (as is often the case for
governments) acted as if it had all of the information and was able
to predict what would happen, particularly in Iraq. Of course in
the end that has not been the case.

The recognition that there will always be unknown unknowns is
one of the reasons why anticipation rather than prediction is the
most effective strategy for dealing with the future.

The other reason for including this quotation is the message that you are unlikely to ever know everything about the situation and thus you need to constantly work on improving your view of the situation. In part this involves increasing the accuracy of your understanding, refining your view of information you already possess. An example of this approach is the refinement that quantum physics brought to physics. Physicists kept measuring, experimenting, and devising new theories to explore and explain the world. Improving your view of the situation can also involve expanding the areas you examine to encompass more and more of the picture. This is the systems approach, which is so important in our interconnected world.

For me one of the biggest ironies of the Rumsfeld quotation is that Donald Rumsfeld was "awarded" the Foot in Mouth award for it, from an organization called the Plain English Campaign, a British organization that strives to have public information delivered in straightforward English. The fact that these people missed the point of what he was saying is not the worst part; worse is that most news organizations just reported the fact that Rumsfeld won the award.

One of the reasons that unknown unknowns exist is because of our filters. In many cases there are clues to the fact that we don't know something, but the clues are blocked by our filters because they are too far out of our normal experience. But, as Rumsfeld said, we eventually discover some of these unknown unknowns either because we look for them or because they slap us in the face, the former being the preferred approach.

Proactively looking for the unknown unknowns is necessary in large part because of two factors: the interconnectedness of our world today, and, due to the large number of people on the earth, the effect we collectively have on the planet. Gone are the times when you could ignore what other countries are doing. Economics, the environment, and limited natural resources are some of the areas where the actions of one society have an impact on other societies.

Similarly, to get the most value from your own planning you cannot ignore the actions of those outside your immediate circle. In fact you have to continually increase the size of the circle from where you draw your information. If you are to get the most utility from the approach of anticipating the future you must continually assess whether you are casting a wide enough net when you gather your information.

The mindset of continually expanding our boundary conditions when we are planning, examining the consequences, and exploring scenarios is what I call "Wholeception." I created a new label for this approach because I felt there was no existing word that adequately described it. The figure on the next page shows the continuum in quality of thinking from being unaware of one's thinking, through Thinking for Results and consequential thinking, to Wholeception. As individuals, groups, or nations become more aware of how they are thinking and making decisions they start taking in more information, looking at bigger pictures and understanding the consequences of their decisions.

As an example, on an individual basis someone who is unaware of their thinking processes and the filtering they carry out has a reactive response in situations. Their thinking tends to be dominated by past habits and assumptions. To move to the next level of truly solving problems and thinking creatively they must understand the role that their filters play in the conclusions they reach. Once they understand the idea of filters they tend to make better decisions because they can consciously modify their filters to take in more information than they otherwise would have. The next level of thinking is the Gedanken step, where people anticipate the future by asking themselves Then What Happens?

Manifestation

Unaware...........Thinking for Results™..........Consequential.....Wholeception™ →

Approach	Compliance with Systems (or noncompliance)	Awareness of Systems	Analysis of Systems	Improvement of Systems	Design of Systems
Organizational Contribution	Contributes labor	Source of information	Recognizes problems	Suggests solutions	Helps move organization forward
Individual	Reactive responses Habits Assumptions	Problem solving Creative thinking	Decision making	Strategic thinking	Scenario exploration
Group	Conflict Missed potential Silos	Communications Active Listening Influencing Getting Unstuck	Cooperation Customer relations Teamwork	Efficient allocation of resources	Organizational mission Branding
Global	Conflict Unsustainable	Societal understanding	Acceptance of others	Effective international interactions	Global cooperation

Finally, Wholeception is the stage where an individual doesn't simply take past experiences and existing information and extrapolate to the future, but creates alternative scenarios for the future that can be explored and analyzed for their impact.

When we look at the quality of thinking required from our leaders these days, especially in view of the interconnection of our world, we need people who are applying Wholeception to their situations. But too often we find people who, at best, are at the strategic thinking level. They may ask Then What Happens? but they are basing their decisions on information from a limited view of the past and present. Although this may result in an efficient operation for their world as it exists in this moment, this limited worldview produces organizations and institutions that don't last. Of course, as I discussed earlier, in many cases this type of short-term, limited worldview is what the financial market is asking for from our leaders. It is also often what citizens are asking of their governments.

When it comes to relations on a global scale, we see a wide range in quality of thinking. I'm afraid that several of the world's leaders operate at the "unaware" level of quality of thinking. Unfortunately they are sometimes the leaders of dominant countries. They spend considerable effort defending their particular ideology, using approaches that may have worked in the past but are not effective now.

As I mentioned earlier, strongly standing up for a position is a characteristic that we look for in leaders. In uncertain times this gives the impression that the leader knows what is happening, where the situation is headed, and has a plan for the future. In recent times there also seems to be more focus, driven I believe by the media, on the leader rather than a team approach to leading.

Yet in uncertain times and complicated situations a leader who understands the limitations of their knowledge, recognizes the uncertainties of their information, and seeks council from others — especially others with different filters — is less likely to create a fiasco and more likely to create a positive legacy.

Chapter 14

Future Preparation with Scenario

Exploration

Near the beginning of the book I made a distinction between anticipating and predicting the future. In this chapter I'm going to present an approach you can use as a framework for anticipating the future. I call it scenario exploration; others call it scenario planning.

As discussed earlier, a goal of trying to predict a single future is asking for failure. The number of factors and variables that affect the way the future evolves makes predicting the future akin to predicting the weather. But, like predicting the weather, there are tools and approaches you can use to minimize the surprises and allow you to be prepared no matter which future unfolds.

I expect you probably already use some of these techniques when you plan for the future. This chapter describes what might be a more structured and expansive process than you currently use. It is designed to give a broader view than most people typically take when planning for the future. In that sense it is related to Wholeception; scenario exploration encourages you to seek out and assemble information into broader views.

Recall the diagram from the chapter on looking forward. At that time I was outlining the utility as well as the limitations of extrapolating from the past to create a view of the future. History is full of discontinuities, of events and inventions that caused major shifts in the path of society. Sometimes these shifts seem to come from out of the blue. In other cases the events or inventions may be extrapolated from current situations, but their ultimate impact is not immediately obvious.

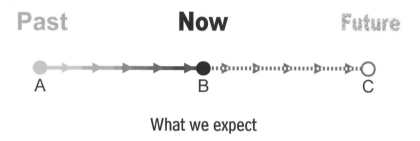

What we expect

Looking at the next figure we can see that though extrapolation only leads in one direction there are many possible futures that

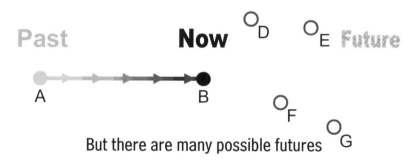

But there are many possible futures

might unfold from the present. As is the case with weather prediction, the further ahead we look the greater the divergence between the different possible futures. I can be pretty confident that tomorrow will be very similar to today, and that not too much will change by next week. But in looking a year or a decade into the future the range of possibilities is vast.

So, how can you anticipate what might happen in a way that is useful for you? How can you develop strategies that will contribute to your organization's success in an uncertain future? How can you develop strategies for your personal life so that you are prepared for the different directions that the economy and society may take? In all cases, how can you identify opportunities at an early stage? Conversely how can you insure yourself against the major risks facing your life?

There are no guarantees personally or professionally. But I do think it is worth investing your time to examine alternative scenarios as to how the future might unfold so you can prepare yourself no matter what happens. The biggest benefit can come from examining scenarios that you initially think might be unlikely — and as a result have never considered — but that could have huge impacts on your situation.

When looking to the future, a tempting question (and the request from many people, especially the media) is "When is ___ going to happen?" Sometimes it is framed slightly differently, for example "What will ___ be at the end of the year?" Trying to answer this type of question can be time consuming, frustrating, and lead to loss in credibility if your answer turns out to be incorrect. Since many of the important issues that might affect your organization or your life cannot be predicted accurately in time, creating plans based on time specific events will often result in inefficient approaches. It is like booking a time and location for your wedding before you are engaged!

I think a more practical technique is to look forward this way:

1. Identify important events and trends which are likely to occur at some point in the future

2. Examine their impact on your situation — will they affect you?

3. If they will affect you, what will your response need to be?

4. How long will your response (if any) take to implement?

This technique of anticipating and planning for the future looks at trigger events rather than trigger times. It works because the more important the event, the lower the need to predict the exact time or date of an event to plan your response. If you estimate that it is going to take your company three years to prepare for a trigger event then knowing whether it will occur four or five years from now (or conversely 12 or 20 months) will not make a significant difference to your action plan. Yet frequently people spend huge amounts of time, money, and energy trying to refine models to accurately predict the future. With the exception of the stock market, in practice it usually doesn't make a big difference.

Another distinction between trying to predict the future and anticipating future scenarios is that because predictions are always looking for the most likely events, they can be blindsided by events that have a low probability of occurring but a high impact. There are areas where most people don't make this mistake; I expect you have insurance of one form or another. I don't imagine you bought your insurance in the hope that you will ever collect on it (and if you did, I don't want to hear about it!). But you are willing to make a financial investment in the insurance to protect yourself against an event that both you and the insurance company hope will never happen.

You may already do some creations of alternative futures in your head. But there are two advantages to approaching scenario exploration in a more disciplined fashion. One, if the scenarios are only in your head, then others can't know about them. By sharing your scenarios you may find others are concerned about the same issues. Or it may be that others have information that can be very helpful as you develop your scenarios. Sharing your scenarios encourages collaboration and is another technique for identifying the elements of your filter.

The second and probably more important reason for formalizing the exploration of scenarios is that if you don't physically develop your scenarios (recording them on paper or in a computer) it is easy for your filters to block important aspects of the scenario. Since your conscious thinking has a limited capacity to hold information, your filter will automatically block some information that seems unlikely or unimportant. But this is often the most valuable information to include in scenario exploration.

The thinking traps described in earlier chapters will also crop up when you are creating scenarios. Often "this has never happened before" will influence your scenario creation. Going back to the analogy of predicting the weather, let's say you are planning a hiking trip close to home during the summertime. At one point during this trip you will be three days away from civilization. Based on your experience and the historical data you have obtained, the weather will be warm. However one scenario, unlikely but possible, is that there might be an extreme cold snap. The question is, should you carry outerwear to prepare for that possibility?

If you are not an experienced hiker, and you try to analyze the situation in your head, your filters will certainly be influenced by your own past history and the weather data you have researched. Since it is extremely unlikely that you will encounter severe cold weather, your brain will naturally want to move along to the next issue. Your filters will block out the next important steps in the examination of the scenario — how dangerous would it be to be caught without a warm jacket? Maybe it would not be dangerous at all; maybe it would just mean lying in your sleeping bag an extra day. Conversely it might be life threatening. If you don't consider the scenario in a more formal way than just giving it a casual thought, it is unlikely you will delve into it deeply enough to gather the required information to make the best decision for that possible future.

When I sailed on a 44-foot boat from Hawaii to Vancouver with the two owners of the boat, there were a lot of scenarios that Malcolm the skipper explored. He thought about what conditions we might encounter and what equipment would be necessary to handle those conditions. Knowing him as I did, I had absolute confidence that he had prepared the boat well. On the trip itself (long before the days of GPS) we kept a rigorous log of our direction and speed for navigation purposes, since we were navigating by sextant and were never sure when it might be cloudy. Even though we were in the middle of the Pacific ocean, and only came across a couple of other boats in the whole three week trip, we always kept a lookout. The odds of colliding with anyone out there were extremely small, but it was not impossible, and the consequences could have been deadly.

So what does scenario exploration look like? I will describe the process in more detail below, but essentially scenario exploration is about creating stories and painting pictures of possible futures. Because you're telling stories, you can tell yourself that your thinking can be fanciful in your creation of the scenarios. By painting rich pictures capitalizing on your imaginative abilities, you can uncover possible trends, ideas, and directions that you might not otherwise identify if you are strictly focused on what is most likely to occur. And the approach of treating each scenario as a story rather than a prediction avoids the mental anxiety that comes with the possibility that your prediction may prove to be wrong.

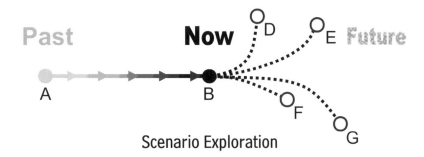

Scenario Exploration

You can also consider situations that you don't want to occur and prepare for them. There is even a common phrase for this type of planning: worst-case scenario. The alternative is to ignore these possible situations and "hope for the best." (Maybe scenario exploration is a way around the "Law of Attraction." If I don't predict something negative will happen but instead write an imaginary story about how it might happen, is it possible to avoid "attracting" the event?)

Many years ago I read a book written about the making of the original *Star Trek* series. One chapter described many ideas that were created on the show, which later became reality. The technology to implement these ideas had already existed, but because the writers of *Star Trek* were not constrained to what was currently thought to be possible or realistic, they dreamt of things that others had not thought of. In *Star Trek* terms, they went where no one had gone before. The reason no one had gone there before was because they had been limited in their thinking to what at the time seemed feasible or realistic.

The storytelling aspect of scenario exploration is an important one. Because your brain is so familiar with today's world, you will constantly be tempted to discount ideas that seem outlandish or fall back on ideas that reflect the status quo. You have to be careful not to fall into the trap of simply extrapolating today's situation and calling it a scenario. On the other hand, scenarios that have no resemblance to reality are not that useful either.

Although you can carry out scenario exploration on your own, you are more likely to create rich, imaginative, and useful scenarios if you engage others in the process. There are two reasons that having a team of people helps with scenario exploration. One is that you get a richer and more diverse set of experiences so that the historical information comes from a broader base. Two, if you have a good mix of people, and cooperation and openness in the room, you are more likely to generate ideas that might otherwise be eliminated by your own expertise and filters before they are incorporated into the scenario. This is analogous to the *Star Trek* story above. For example, if you are someone who is familiar with robotic technology, you may "know" that it is impractical to build a robot that walks up stairs. You would likely (consciously or unconsciously) eliminate that possibility from your scenarios. Someone who is unfamiliar with robots and how difficult it might be to create a robot that can walk up stairs would not carry out the same type of self-censorship of the idea. The final outcome from the scenario exploration might be a compromise, a different approach, or the stair walking might end up being irrelevant to the scenario. But to discount an idea in a scenario because of "that has never happened before" is to slip into a common thinking trap.

I expect you see that the best scenario exploration occurs when you have a team that works together well and that uses the techniques and approaches from earlier chapters. Communicating effectively with each other, embracing diversity, keeping your filters open, and making the effort to understand others' filters will all help with scenario exploration.

Scenario exploration is also most effective when the process is started a long time before decisions have to be made on the issues explored. This allows scenario exploration to be divorced from everyday operational decisions. Part of scenario exploration is the creation of future worlds, almost fantasy worlds. But the foundation for these worlds is actual events and drivers — things that might have been missed in the past because you were not specifically looking for them and thus were blocked by your filters.

The next chapter will provide a specific example of the scenario exploration process.

CHAPTER 15

SCENARIO EXPLORATION IN ACTION

So how do you start to formulate these future worlds from the infinite number of possible future worlds? The most common way is to start by identifying the driving forces that will influence your situation in the future. What are the most important factors that will affect the decisions you need to make right now regarding the future?

Let's work through a simple, specific example. Imagine you are a 28-year-old married man who is going out to buy a new vehicle. And let's create some simple scenarios to look into the future and help you make the decision today. The first step is to identify some of the driving forces. When buying a new vehicle one of the driving forces would be gasoline prices. Now remember we're not going to try to predict gasoline prices; in fact, what we will do is create scenarios that reflect situations in the case of both an increase in gasoline prices as well as a reduction in gasoline prices. Another key driving force would be the amount of space you need. The price of the vehicle is important for most people. Perhaps for you the performance of the vehicle is important, or maybe you would really like a vehicle that will have a high resale value when you decide to sell.

(Note that even at this point some assumptions have been made, principally that you need your own gasoline-powered automobile.

Where I live, in downtown Toronto, more people are choosing to forgo their own vehicle and take transit, walk, or bicycle. On those occasional times they need to carry cargo, they rent a vehicle or take a taxi.)

Sometimes what first appears to be a driving force may in fact have a more important or universal driving force beneath it. The space you need in your vehicle, the price, and safety considerations might all be components of a larger driving force — do you or will you have children during the life of this vehicle?

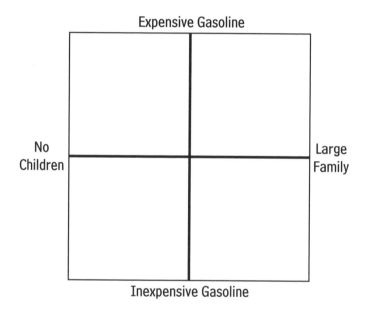

Once you have a comprehensive list of the driving forces you can start to prioritize and whittle down the list. The traditional approach in scenario exploration or scenario planning is to choose two key driving forces and create a four quadrant matrix using these two key driving forces as axes. In the example of buying a new vehicle, one of these axes might be gasoline prices and the other might be the projected size of your family as shown in the figure.

You can now start to construct your scenarios. Remember that the point is to stretch your thinking without creating unbelievable scenarios. So for example, based on your current situation and discussions you've had with your wife, the family size you pick for these scenarios might range from no children to three children. And gasoline prices might range from less than the current price up to two or three times the current price.

You may want to try filling in your own information right now for this hypothetical scenario based on your beliefs, experiences, and filters. When I did this, I came up with the four scenarios labeled in the next figure. These reflect my personal values; for example, I am not someone who particularly likes driving and so I don't place a very high value on the driving experience. I'm not overly concerned with the performance or looks of my vehicle; I

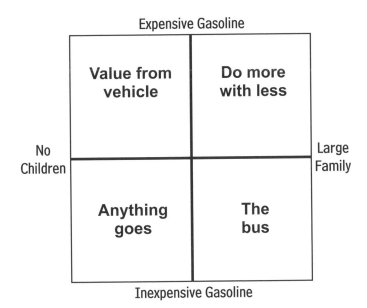

view it as principally a form of transportation. With that in mind, the labels I came up with for the four scenarios I created are "the bus," "do more with less," "anything goes," and "value from vehicle."

To flesh out my descriptions, "the bus" is the future scenario where I have a large family and thus am concerned with carrying capacity, child seats, and safety. Because gasoline prices are low in this scenario I don't need to worry about fuel efficiency. In this scenario a van or sport utility vehicle is a likely choice. (Note that you don't have to agree with this conclusion; I will discuss this in more detail later.)

"Do more with less" is the scenario where I need carrying capacity for my family but gasoline prices are high. In this case maybe a fuel-efficient station wagon would be a good choice.

"Anything goes" allows me to indulge in my fantasy vehicle, since gasoline is low and I have few specific requirements for the vehicle. If I was a performance enthusiast, this might be the quadrant for a muscle car.

The "value from vehicle" quadrant is where gas is expensive but, as was the case with the last scenario, I have a lot of flexibility in what I choose. If I like performance, I might go for a sports car; if not, I might choose a fuel-efficient subcompact.

As you create these scenarios new realizations appear. Sometimes they are an identification of new parameters, and sometimes you identify aspects of your filter — assumptions that you made as you created the scenarios. Some questions that might come up are:

- What is my budget?
- Is total cost of ownership important?
- How many miles or kilometers am I likely to drive in a year?
- Will I drive this vehicle to work or take transit?

- Am I concerned about the environment and thus want low fuel consumption no matter what the price of gasoline?

Some of the realizations may result in you re-labeling or possibly re-evaluating your axes. For example, if you examine the last question and decide you want low fuel consumption no matter what the price of gasoline, then for you the price of gas is not a driving force. It is immaterial in your decision and you should create a new axis and redo your scenarios.

But for now, let's continue with the existing scenarios. One of the most valuable outcomes of scenario exploration is the identification of robust strategies. A robust strategy is one that leads to success no matter which scenario unfolds. A sporty, fuel-efficient station wagon might be a robust strategy in the vehicle example. Or maybe a small, sporty car coupled with a trailer to carry things when necessary. (I have observed this strategy quite frequently in Europe, where fuel prices are traditionally high compared to North America. You see BMWs pulling utility trailers. This is another argument in favor of diversity in the experience and membership of your scenario creation team. The more diversity, the more likely they will know of or create innovative solutions.)

Another benefit of scenario exploration occurs as time passes. Since you have created different views of how the future might unfold at some distant point in the future, as you get closer to that point you will see telltale signs of which of your scenarios is most likely to occur. Looking at the figure on the next page, if down the road you find yourself at the location of the arrow, you can expect that your "E" scenario is the most likely one to occur. You now have a jump on your competitors who are in the process of trying to fit the data they see into a prediction they have made. You can now prepare for E, or even better, refine your scenario exploration based on the new information.

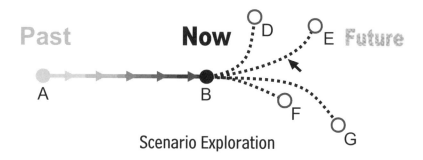

Scenario Exploration

I trust you can see some of the many directions that scenario exploration can take you. In the vehicle example it may raise the question as to whether you need or want a new vehicle or if, in fact, there are better alternatives. Maybe you are also considering moving, and that is another important dimension to the scenarios. If you end up with too many axes, one way to sort out which ones to use in your scenario creation is the paired sort technique. This is described in my first book or you can download a description and a worksheet from www.ThinkingforResults.com.

When it is working to its fullest potential, scenario exploration is useful precisely because it is not trying to predict the future. Possibly the most valuable aspect of scenario exploration is that it provides the process with which to discover more about your own filters. In constructing scenarios you will identify some of your existing filters. By examining the scenarios you create you will open up your filters to new possibilities. And you will avoid some of the thinking traps such as only seeing the information that you want to see. Since the scenarios are admittedly creations of possible futures the process of scenario exploration allows for more imagination and less reliance on "conventional wisdom."

As mentioned earlier, scenario exploration is also useful as a communications tool. Taking the time to develop rich future scenarios helps others to understand the visions you have in your head. It makes it much easier for them to contribute their per-spectives to the scenario. Through deliberate consideration of multiple futures, scenario exploration as a strategic planning tool promotes a realistic examination of possible futures. It furthers both a perceived and an actual increase in your control over the future because rather than hoping that one thing will happen, you are prepared if different things happen. Since you can neither predict nor control the future, being prepared for the future is your best bet.

THE FUTURE APPROACHES
(FASTER THAN YOU THINK)

CHAPTER 16

KEY THREATS LEADERS SHOULDN'T MISS

We live in an ever-more interconnected world. Gone are the days when our actions as societies could be taken in isolation. The sheer number of people on earth, in combination with our ability to amplify the effects of our actions through technology means that many choices we make will result in effects that last for decades, if not forever. These choices require leaders who use decision making techniques such as Gedanken thinking and Wholeception.

With the scale of our actions and the extent of our interactions, one society's actions affect another. International pollution crosses borders; water use upstream affects communities downstream.

International trade has resulted in virtually every resource being traded on a global scale, resulting in global competition. In past decades demand for resources and energy came primarily from the industrialized Western countries. Now the newly industrialized countries have been exposed to the Western marketing machine and their burgeoning populations are seeking to achieve the lifestyles of the West. The growth in demand has helped resource-rich countries, but has also begun to demonstrate the finite nature of these resources. Although some governments (such as Norway's) have been saving some of this one-time wealth and using it to diversify their economies, others spend as if there is no tomorrow to consider. Consuming nations as well seem to be ill prepared for the possibility of shortfalls.

The growth of world trade, and especially multinational corporations, has also increased the interconnectedness of economies. Tensions have increased over the outsourcing not just of labor but also of pollution and energy requirements. As Western economies have moved toward the "knowledge economy" and shifted production to China and other emerging economies, the pollution they produce and energy required for manufacturing have decreased. On the other hand, the countries that have become the workshops of the multinationals have seen the fastest rise in energy demand and rapid increases in pollution and carbon dioxide levels.

The four principal themes of this book — thinking accurately, looking to the future, understanding others, and collaboration — are all required more now than ever before. I believe that it is essential that we as individuals take responsibility for raising our own awareness of the issues in these areas. We need to look at the filters through which we view our world and our actions. We need to look at the consequences of the decisions we make as citizens of the world. We need to look deeply into issues, to use Wholeception, and to encourage this in others and share our knowledge.

We seldom see truly deep analysis of issues; often discussions are positioned as one winner and one loser in the extreme thinking style I described earlier. Media today is a business, and with few exceptions is reluctant to rock the boat very much.

If you are a business leader you have a responsibility to look at the effects of these issues on your own business. Simply extrapolating past events into the future is no longer sufficient when planning business strategy. And for your personal situation, and that of your family, you may have some important decisions to make regarding your lifestyle.

The importance and the challenge of collaboration on a world-wide level has become increasingly apparent. The topics I'm going to talk about in this chapter are all ones where the best solutions require cooperation and collaboration. But the "tragedy of the commons" dilemma has yet to be resolved in most of these areas. (The classic illustration of the tragedy of the commons, as outlined by Garrett Hardin, is that of a community of animal herders sharing a single pasture, the commons. Each herder owns and profits from their own animals, but pays nothing for the benefit of their animal grazing on the pasture. If an animal is added by any herder, the pasture is slightly degraded by the grazing of the additional animal. This degradation affects all herders using the common pasture. But for each individual herder, their benefit increases with each animal they add since they receive all the proceeds from adding an animal whereas the cost of pasture degradation is shared by all. Thus for each and all herders the rational decision is to keep increasing the size of their herd leading to a situation where the commons is overgrazed and collapses. A recent example is the massive collapse of the North Atlantic cod fishery.)

Occurrences of the tragedy of the commons can be reduced through the use of the approaches and techniques I have been describing in this book — anticipating the future, Wholeception, sincere efforts to understand others' positions, and cooperation and collaboration. But acting on any of these techniques requires suspension of a drive for individual short-term profit and instant gratification. That our brains are predisposed to choose a short-term benefit over a long-term one should not be a surprise; in prehistory as our brains were evolving this was probably a necessary strategy for survival. When life is precarious, the inclination to think years in advance is not a great asset. (I am reminded of the joke of the two hikers who stumble across a bear. When one hiker starts running, the other calls out "what are you doing, you will never outrun a bear." The first hiker replies "I don't have to outrun the bear, I only have to outrun you.")

Once again our capacity to affect the world has changed more rapidly than the ability of our brains to evolve. And in this case, the current interconnectedness of our world is a disadvantage, because the evolution of our brains, aside from being a slow process, has no opportunity to develop in different societies. (One can conduct a thought experiment wherein different societies faced with the same situations of constrained resources would result in different brain evolutions such that those who planned ahead, collaborated, and conserved would fare differently from those that only thought in the short term. My expectation, based primarily on reviewing historical societal collapses, is that the societies of long-term thinkers would outlast those of short-term thinkers.)

But the reality is, our brain has evolved to discount the future, and only through rational debate and conscious choices are we able to recognize the value of longer-term thinking. It is hard to overstate the importance of this observation. It is almost akin to an addiction; we have to be constantly and consciously reminding ourselves of the temptation of short-term thinking and instant gratification. Of course, the process is not helped by marketing machines continually trumpeting products that provide instant rewards. Much of the very survival of our businesses, societies, and likely our world in the coming decades will depend on our ability to make decisions that consider the future, not just the present.

The dilemma with the tragedy of the commons can be resolved through big-picture thinking. But what is the big picture, and how can it overcome the mindset of "Why shouldn't I do it, everyone else is?" If the group is small and closely connected, moral suasion may be enough. If they are family members or neighbors, cooperation may come fairly easily. But on world issues where there is no personal connection (where, in fact, there might be historic or cultural divides) appealing to morality is rarely enough, especially in situations where cheaters could prosper.

Cooperation can be encouraged or enforced several ways, or by some combination of the following:

1. Imposed through government regulations.

2. Encouraged by aligning the herders' benefits with the preservation of the commons — for example, a cooperative.

3. Putting the commons under the control of a person or organization in whose interest it is to preserve the commons.

Note that without some action, "market forces" will lead straight to the tragedy. The more astute the herders are, the faster they will act and the faster the resulting decline. The big picture problems discussed in the rest of this chapter all have some element of the tragedy of the Commons.

Growth

The dictionary definition of "growth" contains phrases such as development, becoming more important, unfolding events, the simpler becoming more complex, growing in value, reaching maturity. People grow, physically, mentally, and emotionally. Plants grow. And societies and economies grow.

In the vast majority of uses, growth is taken as a synonym for good. But we have to remember the medical definition of growth: an abnormal proliferation of tissue (as a tumor). In fact there are few diseases that are more feared than cancer — a case of uncontrolled growth.

In society and in economics there are occasionally examples where growth gets out of control, such as communities that expand too rapidly to respond, or inflation that sets commerce on its ear. Still, over recorded human history we have seen a progression of growth because we have not yet hit significant limits to growth on planet Earth.

Eventually our global growth must stop. We live on a finite planet, with finite resources. How many people we can put on this planet is far too complex a calculation to try to attempt. It is highly dependent on the lifestyles assumed for the people. Some say the current population level is not sustainable. Others point to statements from the past that said world population had reached its limit, yet here we are with an even larger population than when these predictions were made.

For a limited time sustainable resources can be harvested at a rate greater than their capacity. But a forest is not sustainable if it is cut at a rate higher than its regrowth rate. Similarly, pollution and waste products released into the atmosphere or the oceans can be absorbed, but at a finite rate. Yet if the focus by businesses, politicians, or individuals is only on the short term, these simple but essential considerations will not be addressed. The mindset associated with Wholeception is necessary to create truly sustainable approaches to resources.

Finally, and most importantly, there are one-time resources that we have mined or pumped out of the ground that will run out one day. I discuss the specific area of energy depletion later in this chapter. We have been extracting minerals from the Earth for a long time and in ever-increasing volumes. At some currently unknown point in the future these too will eventually become more and more difficult to find and extract.

Almost every economy these days assumes that growth is good. While growth itself is not inherently bad, it seems that it is rare today to acknowledge that there might be limits to economic and societal growth. In large part this is because governments themselves have become addicted to growth. Money borrowed today by governments through deficit financing is paid back by future economic growth. Corporations and industries that do not grow are rated as inferior. In industries that seem to have reached their peaks mergers are often used to create growth.

In some circles there is renewed investigation into the limits of growth. Recently several authors have written about why societies have declined in the past — I have included references to several of these works in the bibliography. Many of them point out parallels between current Western society and past civilizations. In my opinion one of the best is *The Upside of Down* by Thomas Homer-Dixon. His research was focused on the Roman Empire and the reasons for its decline. He points out that growth of the society and expansion of the empire occurred symbiotically, in large part because the growing empire required more energy, provided in those days through agriculture. In the end, diminishing energy returns meant the demise of the Roman Empire.

But even in our modern world, is growth always necessary for success? This has become such a pervasive filter in our society that few even think to ask the question and fewer still attempt to answer it.

In the first few years of my professional career I worked for a high-technology company that made very specialized test equipment. Over a period of years I continued to consult with them.

The original owners eventually sold out when they were ready for retirement. Over most of the 25 years of the business when I was involved, employment varied between about 15 and 20 employees. Both the owners and the employees were people who liked what they did — they were interested in technology and enjoyed creating and building products. The company never became a "superstar," but it provided a nice living for a group of people who loved their jobs. The majority of employees worked there longer than 20 years, a rarity these days. This company went against the grain of growth, and yet provided good jobs and innovative products, a good return for the owners, and intellectually challenging employment. In review, it seems to me that looking at it through this type of filter, this was a successful company. But if you look at it through the filter of growth as the principal goal, it was not successful.

Furthermore, I believe that preparing for an economy that is not continually growing will be an important defensive strategy in the next decade. I think that assumptions we have made in the past — that continual growth is not only desirable but the only way to succeed — will be challenged. I realize this is an uncommon viewpoint; but I would argue that most people have not examined their filters. It is impossible to say exactly how the future will unfold, but I do think it is safe to say that prudent people will consider the possibility that the future might look substantially different from the past half-century. Companies and countries that base their success on growth rather than improvement may be in for a shock. If the success of your organization's current plan is based on continual growth, I suggest you investigate some scenarios that do not make the assumption of growth. Use the technique of scenario exploration outlined earlier in this book. How would a change in this assumption affect your strategies?

Energy

In August 2003, Ontario and much of the Northeast United States experienced a total blackout for 24 hours. In California in 2001, people and businesses experienced rotating blackouts. In these situations everything grinds to a halt. Life as we know it in the Western world stops.

Nothing, absolutely nothing, is more critical to the success of every aspect of our modern society then an adequate, reliable supply of energy. From lighting to powering essential equipment, from heating to transportation, businesses, hospitals, home life, police, fire, and rescue services, all rely on energy, especially electricity.

We are facing, in North America and around the world, what I call an energy predicament. I chose the word predicament deliberately. A predicament is defined as an unpleasantly difficult or complicated situation. Note that there is a distinction between a predicament and a puzzle. People like puzzles — look at the popularity of crosswords and Sudoku. But people don't like predicaments, and in fact a common response to a predicament is to ignore it — often while acknowledging the evidence of the problem. (The Ostrich Approach once again.)

Our tried and true sources of energy are aging. Many are not delivering the amount of energy they have in the past. At the same time, worldwide demand for energy continues to increase. The tightening of the relationship between supply and demand led to the increase in energy prices witnessed in 2007 and 2008.

Since energy is so central to the functioning of our modern society — we absolutely cannot do without it — both corporations and individuals will continue to pay ever-increasing prices for energy. When gasoline prices in Canada first reached one dollar per liter I appeared on several radio programs commenting on energy prices. Why was this news? Because $1 per liter was a milestone, unusual, a price no one (looking through the filter of their past experience) had imagined would be reached. One common question was "how high will gasoline prices go?" As is the case for many aspects of the future I don't believe anyone can predict gasoline prices. It is one of those issues where there are too many variables to consider. A more effective strategy is to ask how high could prices go, and how would they affect your situation? One way to anticipate the price that gasoline might reach is to turn the question around and ask "how much will people rationally pay for the comfort, convenience, and time savings of using their own vehicle?"

On our website www.EnergyPredicament.com we have a gasoline price calculator where you can enter parameters such as your vehicle type, the distance you travel, your transit alternatives, and the value you place on your time. The calculator will compute the price you should rationally pay for gasoline. The statistics show a median price of over $7 per liter in Canada and $20 per gallon in the United States. The irony is that those who travel shorter distances and use less gasoline are the ones who could and would pay more, though they are also the ones who typically have the best transportation alternatives. I'm not suggesting that everyone could afford to pay these prices, but that there are many people who will. Gasoline and other energy products are essential to the way that many people have structured their lives and people will choose to forgo other purchases to pay for energy. Moreover, each time prices reach new uncharted territory, most people naturally assume they will come back down, or at least level off. The best thing to happen regarding energy awareness was the steep steady rise in oil and gasoline prices which started in

February 2008. Since the trend was so clear, people could not filter out the reality that something significant was happening with world oil supply.

A good place to start any energy discussion is to put into context our current sources of energy. The next figure shows the mix of our sources of energy worldwide in 2005. The first striking point is that only eight percent of the energy produced worldwide

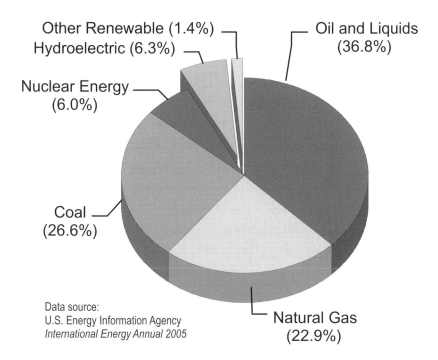

Other Renewable (1.4%)
Hydroelectric (6.3%)
Nuclear Energy (6.0%)
Coal (26.6%)
Oil and Liquids (36.8%)
Natural Gas (22.9%)

Data source:
U.S. Energy Information Agency
International Energy Annual 2005

originated from renewable energy. Of that renewable energy, the large majority came from hydro electricity. So despite all of the talk about renewable energy and all of the activity in that field, the newer renewables such as wind, solar, and biomass still only amounted to about one percent of world energy consumption.

(This perception that renewables form a bigger proportion of energy supply than they actually do is an example of the thinking traps described earlier; news about renewables is both frequent and recent. Also a windmill is a very visible source of energy.)

Oil supplies over one-third of the energy consumed worldwide and provides the large majority of fuel used for transportation. Automobiles, trucks, airplanes, ships, and most trains are powered by liquid fuels derived from oil. A wide range of economic activity, from globalization to the expansion of the suburbs, depends on the consumption of inexpensive liquid fuels.

Natural gas is used worldwide for heating and to a lesser extent for electricity generation. Coal is used almost exclusively for electricity generation, especially in the United States and China.

At some point in the future, as these nonrenewable sources of energy are consumed, the energy from fossil and nuclear fuels will decline. Some will decline faster than others; there may be some regional differences based on the transportation of fuel. But ultimately, if society continues, all of the energy consumption that is currently met by these nonrenewable sources will have to be replaced — either we will have to use less energy in total or we will have to increase the amount of energy produced from renewable sources.

As I have said before, predicting exactly when this will happen is impossible. As a result, some people prefer to take the Ostrich Approach and ignore the problem. They might say "it is not our problem, let those people a hundred years from now figure it out. They will have better technology, they can fix it."

But the review I have done of studies and research carried out by government agencies, independent geologists, oil companies, and others suggests that energy decline will arrive much sooner than most people think. I anticipate that energy decline will be a significant issue within the next decade, and possibly much sooner, especially if we don't start taking significant action regarding energy production and consumption.

This does not mean that we have to substitute or reduce energy consumption by 93 percent within a decade. Oil, natural gas, coal, and uranium will not run out overnight. But as the easy-to-exploit sources are exhausted, the daily production from these fuels will become more difficult and more expensive. To see how this will play out, read on.

Energy Decline

Until I started studying the extraction, generation, and consumption of energy several years ago, I had never really thought about where our day-to-day energy supply comes from. Being a physicist, I understood how energy was generated, transported, and consumed, but I didn't realize the size of the scale involved. Like most people, I flipped a switch and the light came on or I nudged up the thermostat and my house became warmer.

I also didn't understand much about the process of oil and natural gas extraction. If you had asked me "are oil and gas finite resources?"... well, let me ask *you* that question. Are oil and gas finite resources? If your answer is yes, when will they run out? You see, I realized oil and gas were finite, but because I had grown up in an era where both were plentiful and most of the time inexpensive, I had a filter that they would always be there for me. And like most people I had never thought about the future of oil or natural gas.

It turns out that "when will oil and gas run out" is the wrong question to ask. To understand why, we need to take a quick look at the basic structure of an oil field. I had always thought (erroneously it turns out) that oil was in big pockets or pools underground. That is not the case — an oilfield more closely resembles a sponge than a pool. The oil in an oilfield is in pores in the rock.

A good oilfield has very porous rock so that the oil flows easily into a well. A good oilfield also contains oil that is naturally under pressure and thus flows on its own, at least initially.

When an oilfield is discovered the oil company will start to drill wells. Obviously, the wells serve to extract the oil; they also allow the oil company to determine the extent of the oil field. Since the oil is in pores in the rock, it takes a while for the oil to seep through the rock to the well. As a result, the more wells that are drilled, the more oil can be extracted on a daily basis. As the oilfield gets older and the oil is extracted, each well starts to produce less oil. Production can be increased by "squeezing the sponge" so to speak; by injecting water or carbon dioxide into the oilfield to push the oil out.

If an oil field is developed in the way I described above, it will typically have a daily production amount that initially increases, reaches a peak or a plateau for a few years, and then starts to decline. The shape of the rise, the peak, and the decline will depend on a large number of factors such as the type of rock and number of wells. However, every oilfield that has ever been developed has shown this type of behavior. Moreover, when you add up the contributions of a number of oil fields, for example all the oil fields in a country, the sum will show a similar rise, peak, and decline.

The next two figures show examples of these production curves both for oil-producing countries and for an oil field. Currently the majority of the largest oil fields discovered around the world are on the decline side of their production curves. Moreover, many oil-producing countries around the world have passed their peak of production and are in decline. Let me stress again that this does not mean these countries are close to running out of oil, but it does mean they cannot produce as much oil today as they

Average Daily Oil Production by Year
U.S.A., U.K., Norway

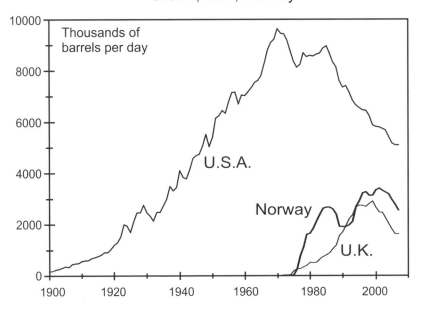

Average Daily Oil Production by Month
Draugen Oil Field, North Sea, Norway

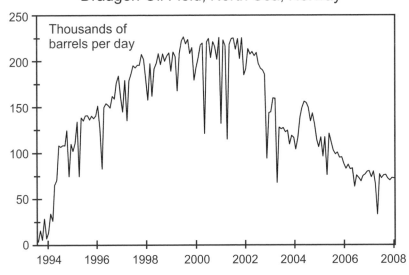

did yesterday. Water injection as described above can be used to slow the decline, but as you can imagine the more water that is injected the less oil that is extracted. There are two limits as to how far you can go with this process. The first is the economic limit — it costs money to pump water into the ground, pump the oil-water mixture out, and separate the oil from the water. The cost to complete these processes must be less than the price received for the oil extracted or the producer will lose money. In other words, when the extraction cost of a barrel of oil becomes greater than the selling price of a barrel of oil, you stop producing from that field. Clearly this economic limit shifts according to the price of oil, so that older fields that are not economical if oil is $30-per-barrel may be economical for $100-per-barrel oil. The second limit is the energy limit — when it takes more *energy* to pump the water down, pump the mixture out, and separate the oil from the water than the energy in the extracted oil, no oil price is high enough to justify continuing to produce from this oilfield. (One small caveat — if the energy used to extract the oil comes from a different source, say nuclear energy, the advantage stemming from oil as a liquid fuel may mean it makes sense to continue to extract the oil even if you lose energy in the process.)

The concern of many people, myself included, is that it appears we will soon reach the point where we cannot increase daily oil production; where, in fact, it will start to decrease. Although there is much debate about when this might occur and how the decline the might play out, there is certainly no disagreement that easy, conventional oil is past its peak and is declining at a rate of a few percent per year. Currently other sources, such as Alberta's oil sands, Venezuela's heavy oil, and deep offshore oil have been able to make up for the declines. But these so-called unconventional sources tend to be difficult to produce, limited in their ultimate daily amount, and very expensive. Even if they could replace the inevitable declines of the much less expensive to produce conventional oil, they would still result in higher average oil prices.

The next table shows production numbers from the top 30 oil-producing countries around the world within the past 40 years.

Daily Oil Production
All time top 30 daily production

Thousand barrels daily Source: BP Statistical Review	Peak year	Production at peak	2007 Production	Percent decline from peak	Notes
USA	1970	11,297	6,879	39%	
Venezuela	1970	3,754	2,613	30%	
Libya	1970	3,357	1,848	45%	
Kuwait	1972	3,339	2,626	21%	
Iran	1974	6,060	4,401	27%	
Indonesia	1977	1,685	969	42%	
Iraq	1979	3,489	2,145	39%	
Other Europe & Eurasia	1983	12,938	456	96%	
Russian Federation	1987	11,484	9,978	13%	1
Egypt	1993	941	710	25%	
Argentina	1998	890	698	22%	
United Kingdom	1999	2,909	1,636	44%	
Colombia	1999	838	561	33%	
Australia	2000	809	561	31%	
Norway	2001	3,418	2,556	25%	
Oman	2001	961	718	25%	
Mexico	2004	3,824	3,477	9%	
Malaysia	2004	857	755	12%	
India	2004	816	801	2%	
Saudi Arabia	2005	11,035	10,413	6%	2
Nigeria	2005	2,580	2,356	9%	
Algeria	2005	2,015	2,000	1%	
United Arab Emirates	2006	2,971	2,915	2%	
China	-	3,743	3,743	-	
Canada	-	3,309	3,309	-	
Brazil	-	1,833	1,833	-	
Angola	-	1,723	1,723	-	
Kazakhstan	-	1,490	1,490	-	
Qatar	-	1,197	1,197	-	
Azerbaijan		868	868	-	

1. After 1987, Russia's output dropped to 6,169 bbl/day in 1999. In 2000 it started to rise, reaching 9,978 bbl/day in 2007. In 2008 it is expected to show a very slight increase.

2. Saudia Arabia's output has varied in a narrow range since 2005.

(Go to www.EnergyPredicament.com to view an illustrative animated map of this data.) The trend in the majority of countries is clear; in 2007, 7 of the 30 top producing countries or regions had their highest extraction ever, while 23 of the 30 countries or regions were below their peak daily extraction levels. No one can predict exactly what will happen to the 7 countries, but with a few possible exceptions, we can anticipate that most of the 23 will continue to decline.

In North America we are seeing a similar situation with conventional natural gas production. Statistically, one is more likely to find the larger, higher-producing gas fields first. Later discoveries tend to be the smaller fields with lower maximum production. Natural gas is much more difficult to transport across oceans than oil, although liquefying natural gas for transportation can be used. However, the volume that can be transported in the near term is small and there is world competition for natural gas.

So oil and natural gas supplies are getting tight. The evidence is there for all to see in two-foot-high numbers at every gas station. You may already have been aware of this, especially if you follow energy prices. But there is another important aspect of the energy situation, one that I haven't seen other commentators addressing. It is common to look at sources and uses of energy in isolation, but as energy pricing changes we need to consider the interrelationships between different sources and types of energy.

For example, recently in North America we have seen large advertising campaigns stressing the need to conserve electricity. A common message encourages us to switch to compact fluorescent light bulbs. Let's put all of this in perspective. The following figure shows electrical, heat, and transportation energy that might be consumed in one day by a family living in a suburb of Toronto. The leftmost bar shows the total of all electricity consumption in

Average Daily Household Energy Use

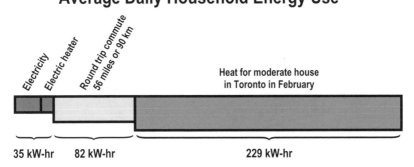

35 kW-hr   82 kW-hr   229 kW-hr

the household. This includes lights, refrigerator, appliances, the furnace fan, computers, and so on. Also shown is the amount of electricity drawn by a single electric heater running for eight hours.

The next bar shows the amount of energy in the gasoline burned for a round-trip commute of 56 miles (90 kilometers). Finally, the last bar shows the amount of energy in the natural gas burned to heat an older house in Toronto in the winter.

In some cases we can switch fuels if one is a lower price than another. For example, in the past two decades many people in North America have switched from electric heating and hot water to natural gas. This has had the effect of slowing the increase in demand for electricity, a result that electrical utilities have not just applauded but generally banked on, as it has allowed them more time to expand their capacity to meet projected demands. However, in the fall of 2005, after Hurricane Katrina disrupted a significant amount of natural gas production from the Gulf of Mexico, the price of natural gas rose significantly when central Canada and the northeastern United States experienced an unseasonably cold November and December. The next figure shows a calculation of the price to heat with electricity compared to the

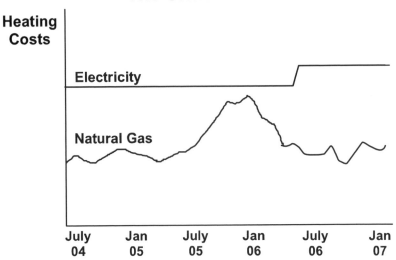

The Critical Issue

price to heat with natural gas in Ontario over this time period. We almost reached the point where it would be cheaper to heat with electricity than with natural gas. Though it probably would not pay to convert your whole heating system, it would be very easy to save money by going to the local hardware store, purchasing a few electric heaters, and plugging them in to reduce the amount of natural gas you used.

Fortunately for the electric utilities, we never quite reached the crossover point. Because think of what would happen if we did — even one electric heater running 24 hours a day would double most people's electricity consumption. So much for compact fluorescent bulbs! That type of increase in consumption would cause a severe strain on the electrical system. The only possible solution out of the dilemma would be for an instant increase in electricity rates to discourage the use of electric heat. Unfortunately, many if not most electrical utilities seem to be ignoring this scenario.

There are two big challenges to dealing with energy decline. One is that many of the possible solutions will take a long time to implement. Improving public transit is one key way to reduce oil consumption but this approach takes time. Others, such as better building standards, retrofit programs for insulation, and civic planning for lower energy use also have long lead times. But an even bigger barrier is the way people think. The combination of "it's never happened before" with lower emphasis on long-term thinking and higher emphasis on reacting rather than planning means that it may take a significant energy event to wake people up to the situation. It is a complex issue, and yet there are things you can do to prepare yourself and your business for the changes ahead in the energy situation.

Scenario Exploration and the Energy Future

The uncertainty associated with the future of energy makes it tempting to ignore the possible consequences. But the scenario exploration process described earlier can be used to help create strategies that will minimize the downside risk and possibly provide competitive advantages. This section is designed to stimulate your thinking and help start your scenario exploration in the area of energy impact.

Before I delve into the obvious area of energy prices and their effects, let's look at energy supply. I talked before about the situation where people would be prepared to pay much more for gasoline than they are currently paying. I can imagine scenarios where the traditional effect of supply and demand on prices for energy breaks down. It is conceivable that we could see situations similar to those that occurred back in the 1970s, where people lined up for gasoline. Similarly, if natural gas prices were to skyrocket it is unlikely that electricity distributors could react quickly enough to fuel switching to prevent some local overloads of the electrical system. Thus I think it is prudent to have some plans to deal with (at a minimum) short-term energy shortages.

Those of us who live and work in cities have grown accustomed to expect 100 percent availability of electricity and other fuels. But even a short term loss of power can extract a significant cost in lost productivity. As well, many small- to medium-sized businesses may not have good backups and contingency plans. Is your computer data backed up in the event of a power failure? Will your telephones work without electricity? If yours is a national organization you can distribute some of the functions across the country and reduce your exposure to a local energy problem. In a world with global customers can you serve those customers if your local utility is having a problem?

In looking at energy prices we can roughly categorize the impact of energy price increases in terms of direct effects, secondary effects, and tertiary effects. This doesn't necessarily mean the magnitude of the effect; in some businesses the tertiary effect can be the most important.

By direct effect I mean direct business cost increases due to higher energy prices. For many businesses there would be no significant effect from a doubling of electricity and/or heating costs. Those in service businesses or the financial sector typically have utility costs that are a small portion of their expenses. Those for whom direct effects would be significant might include grocery stores (with small margins and large electrical bills), steel and concrete manufacturers (with large energy costs), and households where electricity and heat form a significant part of household budgets. In the transportation sector trucking companies and airlines are directly affected by higher fuel prices. How about your company and your industry? Do you even know how much your organization spends on different forms of energy?

Secondary effects come in two flavors. One secondary effect results from your suppliers having increased costs. For example, if you ship a lot of physical product then higher transportation costs due to higher energy prices will affect your bottom line. The other is a reduction in your business if you have to increase your prices due to higher energy costs. Airlines and trucking companies are faced with this effect. One solution, which works in the short term, is to add a fuel surcharge to your bills. If your customers understand and accept that a fuel price surcharge is linked to a temporary, unexpected rise in energy prices they may not complain too much. (Your customers' acceptance of a "surcharge" will depend on whether it is directly related to the price of fuel and as result goes down as well as up.) But these days most people are accepting that fuel prices are likely to remain high and thus dealing with high fuel costs is a regular part of running your business. Your customers don't get to add on a "surcharge" when their employee wages go up; I expect they will start to feel that you should be able to anticipate and manage your expenses as well as they do.

Once again the "it has never happened before" thinking trap can prevent airlines and trucking companies from seeing the reality of the situation. Sometimes people will assume that their customers will simply accept higher costs. But customers can and will find alternatives. Teleconferences can be used instead of travel. Rail shipping can be used instead of trucks. Of course this does mean the customer changing the way they do business. But companies looking at future scenarios will certainly include higher energy prices and may decide that in the long-term it is worth making the effort to change.

The same logic applies to any organization that has large energy-related expenses. To really prepare for the future you need to look at your customers' alternatives. Do you have competitors that aren't as vulnerable to high energy prices? To ask this question you need to use Wholeception, widening your gaze beyond those you usually consider as your competitors, for example teleconferencing as a competitor to airline travel. You may have great relationships with your customers and be dedicated to serving them with your offerings, but in business, if they see a better or cheaper way of doing things they will likely use it.

The tertiary effects of energy prices will include effects such as lower consumer and business spending. This will likely be reflected in lower discretionary spending, especially on luxury items. Since both short-distance and long-distance travel will be more expensive, customers will want to be closer to where they shop — a factor that will affect both retail locations and the housing market. Not only will drivers look for more fuel-efficient vehicles, but they will likely drive less, resulting in vehicles that last longer. (Besides, who wants to spend a lot of money on something where the key ingredient — fuel — is so uncertain?) The automobile industry will continue to face challenges.

I imagine you get the picture. The prudent course is to use broad-based scenario exploration to identify vulnerabilities and then plan strategies to address the vulnerabilities. It is helpful to get an outside perspective for this exercise — either a facilitator with a good grasp of world events or even a group of diverse friends. Maybe an association you belong to can partner with another, different association and create a brainstorming session.

Of course there are opportunities in the energy situation as well. The obvious one in the long-term is sustainable generation. In the short term, scenario exploration might also identify opportunities such as backup power sources and energy efficiency. Locating near transit or a rail line could pay off as well.

There are no certainties about how the energy situation will unfold in the next couple of decades. I expect we will see a lot of turbulence. I do know, having worked in technological fields, that even solutions that are already identified, approved, and under-taken usually take much longer than expected to implement. I also know that unlike financial extrapolation, geological extrapolation has a physical basis behind it. Oil fields inevitably decline; most around the world are already in that state. I know that in the long term, renewables are the only possible energy source. And my observation is that while pleasant developments usually take longer than we expect, the unpleasant future arrives sooner than we would like.

Climate Change

If you want an example of the impact on your message of the words you choose, you have to look no further than "climate change," often referred to as "global warming." Here in Canada, as in much of the United States, the majority of the population would be happy to see a warmer climate. (I'm writing this looking out a train window at our last big dump of snow!) I can't think of anyone — even environmentalists I know — who hasn't made at least one joke about the advantages of global warming!

Semantics aside, concern about climate change has spread around the world, and I believe for good reason. I don't know if the science is overblown or exaggerated, but scientists tend to be a fairly cautious group. The reputation of science is very important to scientists and I don't see any motivation for them to exaggerate the problem. The only possible motivation I can think of would be for the fame and attention, but the scientists I have known are not really interested in fame and attention — these people are not Paris Hilton.

The challenge for scientists is that, once again, politicians, the media, and to some extent the public want a single definite prediction of what will happen. At this point scientists don't know exactly what will happen and because of the uncertainties cannot professionally make that prediction. Climate change deniers, on the other hand, seem to have no problem making absolute statements.

I believe the way out of the impasse about climate change action is the "precautionary principle." The European Union describes the precautionary principle thus: "The precautionary principle applies where scientific evidence is insufficient, inconclusive or uncertain and preliminary scientific evaluation indicates that there are reasonable grounds for concern that the potentially dangerous effects on the environment, human, animal or plant health may be inconsistent with the high level of protection chosen by the EU."

This goes back to the idea of looking ahead and anticipating the future. It is the idea of insurance. It seems to me to be ludicrous to claim that we cannot take action on climate change because there might be a few percent drop in gross domestic product. What humans are doing with the atmosphere is an uncontrolled experiment, with irreversible consequences. There is no undo button. If there is even a 1 percent chance of climate change happening, then we must do something. What happened to the old saying "look before you leap?"

To those who say that the Earth has gone through natural cycles of heating and cooling I say "that is fine, but it is not something we can control." The way man-made actions augment natural climate change is something we can control. Ironically, though I have no children, I think it is our moral duty to do what we can to ensure we don't screw things up for future generations.

Of course, as a moral issue (as Al Gore puts it), it is tough to get traction in a world where economic interests are so prominent. But there has been progress in that regard, and I'd like to now shift gears and talk about the practical, business consequences of the climate change movement.

Climate Change and Business

Whether or not you believe in climate change, it is having an effect on the worldwide debate between and within governments. However, I am still confused as to why the debate about climate change is more visible than the debate about energy decline since energy decline has the potential to hit much sooner, with much larger immediate economic consequences, and less obvious solutions. Come to think of it, maybe that is precisely why it has not received much attention. The old Ostrich Approach rears its head, so to speak. Or maybe it is not a coincidence that the governments who are furthest ahead on climate change — that is, those in Europe — do publicly recognize energy decline and see the overlap between the solutions for both. I do admit it is often easier to motivate citizens to move toward something (action on climate change, alternative energy) than away from something (using less energy, giving up a car.)

Forward-thinking business leaders, even in North America where governments have often been obstructionists on climate change, are recognizing that people in their roles as both citizens and customers increasingly want action. People will alter their purchasing habits or their votes based on what they perceive is being done. Sometimes the net benefit of the action is questionable, but the important thing to remember is that it really doesn't matter — if it affects you, it is important to consider. As an example, cities and countries around the world are increasingly banning one-use plastic bags. I have read white papers (written by the plastic bag industry) that argue that their product is no more harmful than the alternatives. It is a debate that seems to me to have no obvious winner — it depends largely on how the debate is framed. Nevertheless, the movement to ban plastic bags is spreading. If you are in the plastic bag business, it is real, and it is having an effect.

Moreover, I anticipate this will spread to other aspects of the packaging industry. The prevalence of one-use plastic packaging and styrofoam in retail packaging makes their reduction or elimination a logical next target. And there is a very simple way for consumers to take action — after they purchase the product, they can remove it from the packaging and leave it for the retailer to dispose of. In Toronto, we are soon going to be charged by the amount of garbage we put out each week. I am not going to pay to get rid of useless packaging!

The flip side of climate change action is that it provides an opportunity to get ahead of the curve, to be seen as a leading corporate citizen. How much does your business spend on donations? How much positive press does it get you? Have you considered initiatives that save energy, reduce greenhouse gases, save money in the process, and get positive publicity for doing it? If you are a bank looking for a place to invest your billions of dollars and get a reasonable rate of return, how about a program to increase the energy efficiency in your own branches? The benefits include consistent payback, an increasing return on the investment, and the publicity of acting as a good corporate citizen.

Taken together, by employing the precautionary principle, your business can address the moral issue, defend against being singled out by an environmental group, be more prepared for energy decline, save money, and obtain good publicity. It seems to me it would be foolish not to start your climate change plans now.

Public Versus Private

I started my own business over 20 years ago. I am not a stranger to the business world, nor biased against the idea of companies making profits. However, I do think there are some functions that governments are better at providing. In most Western countries basic health care is a publicly provided service.

Even as there is more call — at least in North America — for private industry to provide services traditionally provided by governments, we have the phenomenon of less long-term thinking from corporations. The challenge from a systems point of view is that politicians are elected for relatively short terms but need to make decisions that often have long time horizons, for example infrastructure. If the program is provided by a government body there is a continuity beyond the current politicians. On the other hand, if private industry is contracted to supply the good or service then the temptation is to make short-term decisions based primarily on price.

To continue on the theme of time horizons it is interesting to note that in general, the government with the longest time frame is local government. They are the ones responsible for civic planning and zoning issues. With respect to the issues discussed above, such as energy use and minimizing emissions, the decisions made by local governments will have the largest and most long-term impacts. They are the ones to determine where the buildings that may stand for decades will be located. They also set building standards and codes that will determine the energy efficiency and energy consumed over the lifetime of these buildings. Although they sometimes receive funding assistance from other levels of government, it is the local governments that determine transit planning, for example. The next level of government, state and provincial governments, tends to have medium-term time frames, and focuses on projects such as the construction of highways.

Ironically, national governments that are often considered to have the most power are the ones that generally respond to short-term issues. While things such as economic policy and responses to inflation or recession are undoubtedly important, they typically have an impact over a few years, not a few decades. One area of long-term influence where national governments can and sometimes do act is in the setting of regulations. One of the most successful initiatives in reducing energy consumption has been the Corporate Average Fuel Economy or CAFÉ standards for automobiles. But it is only recently, two decades after they were first introduced, that the CAFÉ standards were tightened by the U.S. government.

It seems that politicians are increasingly reluctant to stand up and propose new regulations. It is not that there are not precedents. Mandatory helmet laws for motorcycle riders and the smoking and drunk-driving initiatives mentioned earlier are examples where governments have acted by considering the long-term public good. Maybe the politicians we are electing these days are just too chicken to take a stand. A small portion of their reluctance to act may come from the legitimate concern that if they don't turn out to be completely right the media will label them as wrong. But not acting on these important issues will, I believe, prove to be even more wrong in the long term.

While I was editing this book, I participated in the Energy2100 conference where I met Gordon Lambert, Vice President, Sustainable Development for Suncor Energy Inc. In a post-session chat, Gord mentioned a phrase which helped me realize I had fallen into the "extreme thinking" trap I described earlier. We were lamenting the lack of long-term thinking that seems prevalent these days, and he talked about "societal projects" — big projects that don't pay off for decades but provide a significant benefit to society. One example we discussed was the building of the Canadian Pacific Railway across Canada in the 1880s. Using today's thinking, is there any government or corporation that would take on that project? Other examples could be the building of national electrical grids or even development of the oil sands itself, which started in earnest 40 years ago.

I realized that in writing the heading for this section, "Public Versus Private," I had ignored the possibility of other options besides the extremes of public or private. Note that the examples above are all much bigger projects than the currently popular "public–private partnerships." The triple Ps are often simply a case of governments contracting out construction or services they would rather not do or finance.

What Do You Do?

As I said at the beginning of this book, I don't believe there is one list of "seven steps to better thinking" any more than I believe there is only one type of problem, one type of solution, or one type of thinker. Effective thinking includes the components I have described — checking your filters, thinking it through, asking Then What Happens. But the implementation and applications of these three components will be different in every situation.

Above all, the first thing to do is to become informed. While you can't be an expert at everything, I do believe for both your personal and work responsibilities it is important to have an idea of the seminal issues of the day. Talk with other people who have researched the topics. Exchange information, and if you find something you believe is important for others to know then talk about it. I think we need more reasoned dialogue these days, especially regarding the challenging issues we face. That is why I started to educate myself on energy issues.

Get involved politically. Vote. Go to all-candidates meetings, and ask questions. Write letters to politicians; it does make a difference. Volunteer for a political party, or maybe run yourself.

Look at the steps that you and the organization you work for can take to address some of the major issues we face. I'm reminded of the old saying "If you find yourself in a hole, the first thing to do is to stop digging." We don't have to do it all right away, but we do have to stop digging and start taking steps. And there are many simple steps you can start to do right now. For the most up-to-date discussion of these issues, visit the website of this book at www.ThePredictionTrap.com.

Conclusion

Most people are pretty good at thinking. My goal in writing this book is not to imply that everyone thinks badly, but to point out the occasional but important areas where we all get tripped up. I hope I have stimulated your thinking and that you will not only ponder some of the issues and approaches I have presented, but talk to others about them. After all, collaboration is a key part of this approach.

As one final thought provoker, in the last chapter I will leave you with a fable. Good thinking!

CHAPTER 17

A FABLE

Consider this story:

Bill had some struggles in his life. He didn't come from a wealthy family, and he couldn't afford to go to college. He didn't have a lot of ambition and survived by taking menial jobs most of his life.

Then one day Bill received a letter in the mail. The letter said that Bill had inherited $200 million from a long-lost uncle. He could not believe his good fortune. That money would allow him to do all of the things he always wanted to do. He read the letter, and it had some complicated language about how the money would be distributed. But Bill wasn't worried about it, because in the envelope was a check for $500,000. Bill had never seen so many zeros! There was also the name of the lawyer who was the trustee for the account. Bill called the trustee, who confirmed that Bill would receive a certain amount of money every month. The trustee suggested that they meet so he could explain the situation to Bill, but Bill wasn't interested in the details.

Since Bill had never had a lot of money, he was not in the habit of spending a lot of money. So when this windfall arrived, he started by buying himself a few new clothes, a car, and a modest house. The monthly checks were more than enough to cover his living expenses.

As time went on, Bill started to become accustomed to having easy money. He didn't bother to shop carefully; he didn't need to. It didn't matter if he wasted a bit, after all, his total inheritance was $200 million. His taste for the finer things developed. He dined in nicer restaurants, bought better wine.

In fact, the monthly allowance was starting to become a limit on his lifestyle. So Bill called up the trustee, and told the trustee he'd like to have more money per month. The trustee once again tried to explain the complexity of this inheritance, but Bill wasn't interested in the legal mumble jumble. "Can you increase the amount I get per month?" asked Bill. "Yes, I can," said the trustee, "but because of the way the inheritance is structured only some of the money can be accessed easily. Other large parts of the inheritance are tied up in different investments and trusts. You can access these funds, but only at a much lower rate each month."

The trustee talked some more, but Bill got bored with all the words and came back to what he called about in the first place. "Just increase the amount I get per month, please," said Bill.

Time passed. Bill was enjoying the good life, and one day he met the love of his life, Cindy. They got married, and shortly thereafter had a baby boy. Life was good.

One day, the trustee called and Cindy answered the phone. Cindy also came from modest beginnings, but Cindy had training in accounting. Unlike Bill, Cindy was interested in how the mysterious inheritance worked. She talked with the trustee for a long time, and when Bill arrived home later in the day she stopped him and tried to explain to Bill how the inheritance worked.

"You see, Bill, part of that inheritance was sitting in cash at the time it came to you. The money you have been receiving over the past several years has come from that cash. It was easy to get at, and, as you have done, it could be increased any time. If we look ahead the end of that easy money is within view. The trustee has instructions that once two-thirds of that easy money is gone, the monthly allowance will decrease every month.

"There is a lot more money left, but as the trustee has tried to tell you several times in the past, it is harder to extract. There is a small amount coming to us right now from these much larger reserves, and it will increase a little bit over time. But that small amount is not going to make up for the decline that we will see from the original cash account in the not too distant future.

"And don't forget, now we have a child. Unless we start to cut back on our extravagant spending, all of this cash is going to be gone before he reaches university. Any monthly income from the much larger, but legally complicated monetary reserves in the inheritance will be too small for our child to be able to go to university and build his own future.

"The way I see it, if we cut back now, then we will have enough resources to be able to send junior to university so that he can develop his own resources and become self-sufficient and sustain his lifestyle even without the income from the inheritance. You have had a very good life, as have I, with this inheritance. But it really is a one-time windfall and I don't think you have been looking ahead very far."

This was not a message that Bill wanted to hear. Bill was very used to having easy money around. Sure it cost some money to pay the trustee, and his bankers, but those were a small fraction of his income. He had been able to spend whatever he wanted, so much so that he had come to believe it was his right. He didn't want anyone, even Cindy, telling him he had to cut back.

Bill was mad. He called up the trustee, and told the trustee what Cindy had said. The trustee confirmed Cindy's analysis. Bill was furious. "I'm going to get someone else look at these numbers," said Bill. "That is your prerogative, but I think you will find that any professional who truly understands the structure of this inheritance will give you the same answer," said the trustee.

But Bill had gotten very accustomed to his lifestyle. Not only that, but he resented the implication by Cindy that if he didn't change the way he was living there would be nothing left for his child. He went looking for another adviser.

In any profession where an "opinion" is part of the service provided, you can usually find someone to say just about anything you want, especially when there is money involved. This case was no different. Bill found someone who told him he didn't need to worry about the future. This person wasn't exactly a lawyer, or an accountant, or a licensed financial adviser. But he did say what Bill wanted to hear. That while it was true that the era of easy cash was over, because there was so much money in reserve, then "we will find a way to get that money out faster. After all, you still have over $180 million left." A little part of Bill's brain was wondering if it really was that easy, but his new advisor kept emphasizing the large amount of money left. "How could there be a problem when you have $180 million in the bank?" said the advisor. Then the adviser asked Bill a question that made him feel much more comfortable. "Have you ever had a problem with this money before?" asked the adviser. "No" said Bill. "Well then why should you start worrying now?" asked the adviser.

The adviser said that his company was continually creating new techniques to extract money from complex trusts. If Bill needed more money, then he had a new "reimburse investment option derivative coupon offering" (or something like that, Bill wasn't really listening) that would allow Bill to extract more money. Of course it would involve some higher fees to pay for the adviser's service, but that was the price to be paid.

Bill signed up with this new adviser. A few more years passed. Occasionally Cindy would bring up the issue of the inheritance because she knew they hadn't cut back. She wondered what might happen in the future. Bill would just tell her that things were being handled, and not to worry, the money was still being produced.

Then one day Bill opened the mail and was shocked to see that his monthly check was only half as much as he expected. He yelled at Cindy "what is going on?" Cindy explained that this is what she had been trying to tell him for years — the easy money had been declining, and though there were still large reserves of the inheritance, they were the type which could only be extracted very slowly. "But what about what my adviser said?" asked Bill. Cindy explained that the adviser had been getting more money from the complicated reserves, but that the adviser had been charging much higher fees to do that. And since each additional dollar was even harder to extract, the adviser charged even higher fees on the most recent withdrawals.

There is a happy ending to this story. Bill was shocked by the realization that although he had over $140 million in reserve on paper, he simply could not extract it fast enough to support the extravagant lifestyle which he had assumed was his "right." It was true that, if he paid more fees, he could extract more money, but it was a case of diminishing returns. In fact there was a point where it would cost him more in fees than the money returned to him. He realized that despite all these reserves, reserves that he would never use in his finite lifetime, there was still a practical limit on how much income could be produced. Not only that, but he had developed his extravagant lifestyle based on the easy cash portion of the inheritance that came at the beginning.

He now realized that the total inheritance would not run dry in his lifetime. But he also realized he could not spend more in a month than the money that came in that month. That was simple arithmetic, and no matter what Bill wished or the advisor said, nothing could change that fact. The amount coming in was much lower than what he was used to. Finally, he recognized that to ensure that his child would have any sort of opportunity to create his own life — a life that could never be as extravagant as Bill's — Bill had to devote part of his current income for education for his child's future. Otherwise his child would experience the same sort of decline in income. In fact, Bill realized if he wasn't careful about how he used the rest of the easy money and the much smaller income from the tight reserves, junior might be a multi-millionaire on paper but a pauper in day-to-day life.

Of course this is a hypothetical story. But there is a very real parallel between this story and the attitude of most people in North America regarding the world oil inheritance. I could expand the analogy; when Bill starts running low on income, instead of cutting back, he searches for more long-lost relatives. Maybe he finds one or two; but their wealth is nowhere near the original uncle and they have similar conditions on their money. So, while it sounds exciting when he first discovers a new great-aunt who willed him $1 million, he realizes that the strings attached to the inheritance means that $1 million is only going to provide him with income for a couple of months in the style to which he has become accustomed. It only postpones the problem for a little while.

In the Western world, and in North America in particular, during the twentieth century we built a society (with its infrastructure and economy) that was based on abundant supplies of inexpensive oil and natural gas. Recent rises in the price of oil are not primarily because of greedy oil companies, or dictators in the Middle East, or rebels in Africa. They are primarily because of supply and demand — the market forces that economists are always championing. Chevron Corp. has told us the "era of easy oil is over." The CEO of Total Energy has said he can see no way that world oil production will ever exceed 100 million barrels per day. (In 2007 total world consumption was about 86 million barrels per day; business as usual projections by the U.S. Energy Information Agency suggests that 100 million barrels per day demand could be reached within a decade.) Yet governments in North America continue to ignore the warning signs. Even simple steps that could significantly reduce oil consumption — such as improving vehicle fuel efficiency standards — are ignored.

The question is — what sort of energy inheritance will you leave for your children and grandchildren?

Bibliography

Note: titles marked with an asterisk are more effort to read than the average book but well worth the mental investment.

Ariely, Dan; *Predictably Irrational*
HarperCollins Publishers, 2008. ISBN: 978-006135323-9
Many entertaining examples of the unconscious decisions we make.

Bransford, John D. and Barry S. Stein; *The Ideal Problem Solver: a Guide to Improving Thinking, Learning, and Creativity*
Worth Publishers Inc, 1993. ISBN: 978-071672205-2
An organized approach for problem solving.

Buzan, Tony; *Use Your Head*
Pearson Education, 2006. ISBN: 978-140661019-2
Primarily covers mind mapping, a visual technique of recording, organizing, and creating notes and ideas. Also memory and reading techniques.

Charvet, Shelle Rose; *Words That Change Minds* *
Kendall/Hunt Publishing Company, 1997. ISBN: 978-078723479-9
Very complete coverage of how to understand and influence people by listening to the words they use. Written by a world leading expert on this specific aspect of Neuro-Linguistic Programming.

Debono, Edward; *Six Thinking Hats*
Little Brown and Company, 1999. ISBN: 978-031617831-0
Description of the technique used by thousands of people to utilize all aspects of our thinking ability and increase efficiency of discussions.

Diamond, Jared; *Collapse*
Penguin USA, 2005. ISBN: 978-014303655-5
"Those who fail to learn from history..." Diamond gives diverse examples of societies that failed to look ahead and examine the consequences of their actions. Valuable for those who have a "but it won't happen to us" viewpoint.

Dixit, Avinash K. and Barry J. Nalebuff; *Thinking Strategically*
Norton, 1993. ISBN: 978-039331035-1
Easy-to-read coverage of game theory in various situations. How to out-think your rivals in adversarial situations.

Harvard Business Review; *Harvard Business Review on Decision Making*
McGraw-Hill, 2001. ISBN: 978-157851557-8
Eight articles contributed by leading management thinkers including Peter Drucker and Chris Argyris. Discusses both thinking tools and methods.

Hoffer, Eric; *True Believer: Thoughts on the Nature of Mass Movements* *
HarperCollins Publishers, 2002. ISBN: 978-006050591-2
As the title suggests, discussion of why groups do what they do. A thin book that took me hours to read, as I would read each paragraph and then stop to think about the ideas for two minutes. Stimulating examples, such as how the Nazis were successful in convincing ordinary people to join their cause.

Homer-Dixon, Thomas; *The Upside of Down: Catastrophe, Creativity, and the Renewal of Civilization*
Island Press, 2008. ISBN: 978-159726065-7
Well written and researched, it looks principally at the rise and collapse of the Roman Empire, drawing parallels throughout to current Western society. A warning about uncontrolled growth and the importance of energy decline.

Jones, Morgan D.; *The Thinker's Toolkit: 14 Powerful Techniques for Problem Solving*
Crown Publishing Group, 1998. ISBN: 978-081292808-2
Fourteen practical processes for solving problems.

Klein, Naomi; *The Shock Doctrine: the Rise of Disaster Capitalism*
Knopf Canada, 2008. ISBN: 978-067697801-8
Looks at how during times of rapid upheaval or shock, people are confused and susceptible to actions by those in authority that they normally would question. Gives many examples where this has occurred.

Martin, Roger L.; *The Opposable Mind*
McGraw-Hill, 2007. ISBN: 978-142211892-4
Very readable discussion of "integrative thinking" — creating new ideas by resisting the either-or type of decision. Good business examples.

McGahan, Anita M; *How Industries Evolve: Principles for Achieving and Sustaining Superior Performance* *
McGraw-Hill, 2003. ISBN: 978-157851840-1
Addresses the trap that many organizations fall prey to in assuming that there is one type of change. Looks at four trajectories of industry evolution (based on whether core activities and/or core assets are threatened) and provides insights and approaches to deal with each of these four trajectories of change.

Orwell, George; *1984*
Signet Classic, 1950. ISBN: 978-045152493-5
The classic novel about the dangers of relinquishing individual thought in exchange for short-term pleasures.

Park, Randy; *Thinking for Results: Success Strategies*
Aronyd Publishing, 2004. ISBN: 978-097339260-9
The first book by this author, it discusses filters and the model of thinking with a focus on the individual.

Paul, Richard and Linda Elder; *Critical Thinking: Tools for Taking Charge of Your Learning and Your Life*
Prentice Hall, 2000. ISBN: 978-013086972-2
The principles and application of the critical thinking method.

Phillips, Kevin; *American Theocracy*
Penguin USA, 2007. ISBN: 978-014303828-3
Comprehensive discussion of three of the major threats to the American way of life. Well researched and thoughtfully presented.

Pinker, Steven; *How the Mind Works* *
W. W. Norton & Company, Incorporated, 1999. ISBN: 978-039331848-7
Pinker collects research on evolution, psychology, and human behavior in a comprehensive look at both positive and negative aspects of how people think.

Postman, Neil; *Amusing Ourselves to Death*
Penguin USA, 2005. ISBN: 978-014303653-1
Written in 1960, it talks about the dangers of living our lives virtually, in this case by ignoring our individual responsibilities for what our societies are doing. May be even more relevant today, in the digital age, than when it was written in the earlier days of television.

Senge, Peter M.; *The Fifth Discipline: the Art & Practice of the Learning Organization* *
Doubleday Publishing, 2006. ISBN: 978-038551725-6
Excellent discussion of how systems influence our thinking and our outcomes.

Skinner, B. F.; *Walden Two*
Pearson Education Canada, 1976. ISBN: 978-002411510-2
A classic, thought provoking novel about the potential for building a society that is fulfilling for citizens by setting out with that goal in mind.

Taleb, Nassim Nicholas; *Fooled by Randomness: the Hidden Role of Chance in Life and in the Markets*
Berkley Trade, 1988. ISBN: 978-039955000-3
An entertaining look at the propensity of humans to try to make meaning where there may be none; also examples of the prediction trap of extrapolation.

Walton, Mary; *Deming Management Method*
Berkley Trade, 1988. ISBN: 978-039955000-3
Very readable coverage of the work of W. Edwards Deming, the quality guru.

Whyte, Jamie; *Crimes Against Logic: Exposing the Bogus Arguments of Politicians, Priests, Journalists, and Other Serial Offenders*
McGraw-Hill, 2004. ISBN: 978-007144643-3
Eye opening accounts of the ways that "logic" is used to justify conclusions that are anything but logical.

There is rapid change associated with many of the issues discussed in this book. For updates to the information presented here and to share your own insights and viewpoints, please visit the website of this book at www.ThePredictionTrap.com.

INDEX